Freedom Ain't Free

Freedom Ain't Free

My Journey from Pain to Purpose

Katrina Harris

Library of Congress Cataloging-in-Publication Data has been applied for.

Ebook ISBN: 978-1-964014-00-5
Paperback ISBN: 978-1-964014-01-2
Hardback ISBN: 978-1-964014-02-9

Cover design: Anton Khodakovsky, bookcoversforall.com

This book is dedicated to my heartbeats, my forever babies: Jr, Kenneth, Shaniqua, and Janae. You are my biggest blessings from up above, and without you, there would be no me. Because of you, I chose to live and not to give up on life. You guys have gone through so much heartache and pain that was beyond your control, BUT GOD! Because of His grace we are all still here today. Thank you for pushing me to become greater.

Contents

Introduction

We were fighting a war with an enemy we could not see. That was one of three things we knew for certain. The other two were that people were getting sick like never before, and they were dying in record numbers.

Covid-19 had us all working on high alert in the hospital from the moment we walked in the doors until we walked back out. I was required to wear an N95 mask, gloves, and protective gear to do my job as a clinical liaison. I'd go from person to person, making relationships with them, becoming their trusted partner as they figured out what was best for their loved ones—when no one really knew for sure what "best" actually meant.

In normal times, I'd have discussions in person. I'd sit near enough to place a reassuring hand on someone's arm and provide human-to-human contact as they grappled with making decisions under uncomfortable or worrisome emotions.

But times weren't normal. I was still the first point of contact for family members. However, I'd speak with them over the phone, making eye contact through a window as I explained the situation of their loved ones and what their options were. If the patient was lucky and going to live, then I'd inform the family members that the patient would need to be moved to another facility. That they had to go somewhere to safely get weaned off oxygen or a ventilator or maybe have their IV antibiotics managed. If they weren't lucky, well, someone would have to plan a funeral.

That N95 and the protective gear may have helped me stave off the virus. But nothing did anything to protect me from the emotional fallout. Death was all around me as I spoke to people who had to make decisions they never expected to make. I talked to children who may never see their parents alive again and to partners who'd ask me unanswerable questions, like "We've been married for so long. What am I going to do without them?" The worst was when I'd have to speak to crying moms who just wanted to know why God was taking their babies away.

I had my own questions for God.

God saved me twice. Once was when I was sent to prison, and the other time was when I survived an aneurysm. Yet there I was on the front lines in the medical field, seeing people die left and right, while I stood among them in perfect health. God seemed to be saving me again. Why?

I wrestled with that question all throughout the pandemic. But for a long while, I didn't have time to get quiet enough to hear God's answer. Every day, I'd gear up to go into the hospital, and then several hours later I'd arrive back home and basically decontaminate. Because no one had any real answers for so long, I'd call home when I was on my way so that everyone knew to get in their bedrooms and not be near me until after I showered. At home, I'd strip down in the garage, leave my clothes out there, and run naked to the shower in order to keep everyone protected, especially my daughter who has a disability. Though, honestly, if I felt I came too close to a situation in the hospital where I wasn't sure how clean I was, I'd drive home in just a bra with my blouse in the back of my car.

Those long days meant I didn't have much time to spend with my family. Often, after I showered and ate, I collapsed in bed, exhausted, knowing I'd have to get up much earlier than I'd want to the next morning. I didn't want to complain. I knew we didn't have it the toughest. I'd watch the late-night news and see how it was *much* worse in big cities like New York than it was in Dallas. Tears would stream down my face, and more questions for God would come. *Why, God? What is going on? What are you trying to tell us?*

The stress became unbearable. I had nightmares. I fell into a depression. I can't thank my husband enough for getting me to realize I needed to take a break and clear my mind. I knew he was right. I wouldn't be able to help anybody else in the state I was in. So when he said, "Pack your bags. I'm taking you home," I listened.

We played old-school music the entire nine-hour drive from Dallas to El Paso. With no masks on or any other constant reminders of what was happening outside our car, we let those oldies but goodies peel the stress off us layer by layer, song by song. By the time we arrived at my mom's house, at the place I call my sanctuary, I was ready to let myself heal.

My mother, as someone in tune with the concept of energy and with how the earth can heal, put her house together carefully. Walking inside is like being in a spa. You simply cannot feel negative energy when you're in her home. The place was exactly what I needed, and my mom took care of me the way good moms do—she cooked, she listened, she soothed. I'd sit by her feet, and she'd assure me I'd be okay, that everything would be all right. And she sat me in her grounding chair, where I was finally able to release the emotional pain tearing me up inside.

We were only gone a couple of days, but it was long enough for me to return to Dallas restored. I went back to work stronger and healthier. And my mind had cleared so much that I could hear those questions again. They seemed louder than ever.

Why was I here? *Still* here, after all I'd been through?

Few people knew what my life had been like prior to my meeting and marrying my third husband. They only knew the current season of me: the happy, successful, woman who looked like she had it all together in a blessed life. None of them knew my real story.

But what was the point in living the life that I had, if I was only to keep it secret? Why did I go through everything I did—with God watching over me and making sure I came out the other side—only to remain quiet about my journey?

That Myles Munroe quote kept coming to me:

> *The graveyard is the richest place on earth, because it is there that you will find all the hopes and dreams that were never fulfilled, the books that were never written, the songs that were never sung, the inventions that were never shared, the cures that were never discovered, all because someone was too afraid to take that first step, keep with the problem, or determine to carry out their dream.*

Meanwhile, I was seeing evidence around me of people dying with their dreams still inside them, with their unfulfilled purposes and inspirations hidden deep. We all have a time limit on this Earth. We never know when it will be, but we all have an expiration date. I knew that obviously included me, someone God had kept alive more than once through situations where others had died.

So I had to ask myself, was I going to be yet another person who dies with her secret story buried along with her? I was proof positive that anyone could overcome adversity. Was I going to walk in my purpose and inspire others to do the same? Or was I just gonna keep quiet?

I understood that God kept me alive for a reason. He wanted me to tell my story. He wanted me to use it to help others, to inspire them not to give up on themselves no matter what their situation. I realized if I could just change one person, that would be reason enough to risk telling all.

But there was a catch: I had to pay for the freedom to tell my story.

That payment came in the form of courage. I had to get brave enough to do it.

The day I walked out of prison, I thought I was free to live my life the way I wanted to.

But I wasn't really free.

The day I trudged through the mud in a Louisiana cemetery to bury my first husband, I thought I was finally free of the hold he had on me, free of the mental anguish from everything he did to me and my children.

But I still wasn't free.

True freedom means being able to tell my story without worrying whether I'm being judged or caring about what people will think of me.

True freedom means I can look at myself in the mirror and see the worthy human being I am instead of a high-school dropout— actually, a ninth-grade dropout and ex-con.

True freedom means being unshackled from feelings of worthlessness and fear so that I can confidently walk out into the world and openly and honestly share myself the way God wants me to.

That kind of freedom takes the courage to be vulnerable.

I have that courage now. And I know God has kept me alive three times now so that I can tell my story in the hopes of inspiring other women to find their own freedom. Because at the end of the day, I think everybody winds up in some kind of prison, whether that's in their minds or in a literal jail. And the only one who can get us out is ourselves.

The only person who can break our chains is ourselves.

I had to break mine. You have to break yours.

And you can.

Trust me. If I can do it, you can too.

This is my story.

Part 1
The Fairy Tale

Chapter 1
My Normal

Hey, Brat. How was school today?"

"Great! Wanna see my report card?"

Not every six-year-old would get excited over showing a report card to their father, but report card day was payday for my brother and me back in 1982. For every A, we'd get ten dollars. Bs would earn us five. Education was important to my parents, especially my mom, who saw it as a difference-maker: those who got a good education wound up with better lives than those who didn't. The thing my mom wanted for me the most was to have a better life growing up than she did.

What I know now is "a better life" has numerous meanings. For example, when I was very young, you could say I had a great life. Our family looked normal from the outside. We had a comfortable middle-class home that my mother kept spotless. We'd go on family trips to Rhode Island to visit my father's East Coast family. We'd go camping in the wilderness. Our bellies were always full; we always had clean clothes to wear; and we got an education.

I was even a princess. That's how my dad saw me. He'd make me the best breakfast eggs in the world in the mornings. I'd sit on his lap while we watched TV and movies together in the evenings. And

9

he'd tuck me in at night, telling me how much he loved me. He'd take me for rides and introduce me to his favorite artists: Rolls Royce, Al Green, Smokey Robinson, and Lionel Richie and the Commodores. We'd go to the park, just the two of us, or we'd go out for ice cream, and he'd assure me I was his favorite girl. He'd even sing that song from the Manhattans, "Shining Star," and tell me I was *his* shining star, that I was meant to shine.

From that perspective, I couldn't ask for a better man to be my father. I always felt safe. I was always at peace knowing that all was well. I had a fairy-tale life where he made me a little princess.

However, there was a dark side to the man too.

My father, either because of his era, profession, or both, was very strict, and he enforced his rules with his belt. I never felt the stinging kiss of leather against my skin, and I was never the one who got the wrath of the man, but my older brother, Tony, wasn't as fortunate.

If Tony didn't come home by the time the lights came on, my father would track him down wherever he was playing and whoop him in front of his friends, and then continue to whoop him with that belt all the way to our front door. If my brother got in trouble at school, my dad would threaten to come to school, belt in tow, to embarrass him in front of his friends. I really think it was the shame more than the physical pain that hurt Tony the most, and my father knew it.

My father was a coder in the army and did a lot of special assignments for the White House involving computers. My knowledge here is vague—I was young, and his work was sensitive. And what military man shares his work with his young children anyway? After he retired, he launched his own IT business but still contracted with the government.

I was always my father's perfect angel, even though he called me Brat. Somehow, the name sounded loving coming from him. Of course, it helped that I never challenged him. I'd learned from watching my brother what *not* to do, and my father never spoke to me harshly or laid a hand on me.

When my mother, Maria, was twelve, her older sisters, who had already moved from Mexico to the U.S., invited her to come live with them. Originally, she planned to be there for the summer, earning pocket money watching her nieces and nephews, but she never moved back home because the needs for the family were greater. She became a housekeeper. Seven years later, at age nineteen, she met my father. She saw him taking photographs in a park in Las Cruces. The rest, as they say, was history...which is always messier than the way the fairy tale goes.

When they got married, her parents disowned her for marrying a Black man who wasn't Catholic. The match both racially and culturally went against their beliefs. The irony here is not lost on me now, as my mother ended up giving financial support to her family throughout her life and helped eleven family members become legal workers in the States. Eventually, that generosity won the day, and they accepted her chosen husband.

My mother's sister, my *tía* Manuela, and her husband moved in with us for a little while. *Mi tía y tío*. They didn't have any children and treated me like I was their daughter. I never went to daycare when my mother went back to school because *mi tía y tío* were always there for me. *Mi tía* would comb my hair and tell me how beautiful I was. She and *mi tío* would take me with them to go grocery shopping, and they'd take me to beautiful places out in nature or in the mountains. They were two more people who assured me all was right in my world, that I was loved,

That sense of safety extended beyond my childhood home and across the border to my extended family in Mexico.

Mexico

When I was three years old, my mother started taking my brother and me with her on pilgrimages to see her family in Mexico. We'd go to Zaragoza, where we were expected to work. I learned how to peel potatoes and prepare meals on those trips. I'd also help make tacos and sell them from a taco stand my aunts had set up in front of a

Catholic church downtown. As authentic a street taco as you can get! It wasn't all work, though. Afterward, it was always playtime and party time!

We would also visit my mother's family on a ranch in Torreón. They had the best Mexican potatoes and homemade tortillas. We'd drink Coca-Cola with them and think it was the greatest meal ever! Although all the children were tasked with milking the cows and goats and gathering the eggs from the chicken coop, we never really minded. We had ample time to play and be kids. There was often a game of kickball going, or we'd play *loteria*, a game with dried beans, and if we won, we'd get little prizes. We also went horseback riding, and at the end of a long day, we'd be part of a laughing, loving family at a big meal or party.

There were only two things that my brother and I didn't really appreciate in Mexico at first. One was that we had to use an outhouse there, which eventually we didn't care about because we were having too much fun. The other was that the place in Torreon was a working ranch.

Being raised vegetarian as part of my mother's adopted Seventh-day Adventist faith, Tony and I only saw meats when we passed them, packaged and lined up in neat rows, at the grocery store. On that ranch, my uncles slaughtered pigs and cows for the family feasts within eyeshot of the main house. The sight was devastating and made keeping to a veggie diet easy for me.

The trips to Mexico were important to my mother. She'd frequently remind us that she was taking us down there so that we'd never forget where we came from. "You'll always have family there, and I never want you to think you're better than them because of your life in America." So she'd pack us up, and we'd ride a bus for several hours. You'd think we hated it. The bus ride was grueling and when we'd finally arrive at our cousin's home, about ten of us would be squished into a house the size of a modern American kitchen. We'd heat the place with a space heater and take a bath with a hose. Then there was that outhouse.

All that was hard coming from a middle-class American life. But we never complained. We learned to value our family. We learned to have the best times of our lives despite the circumstances.

The visits to Mexico weren't the only way my mother remained tied to her family. We kids didn't know it at the time, but she also sent money to support them. Because she had a solid roof, lights, and heat, her family considered her rich. I now realize that is one of the reasons my mom is so frugal. To this day, she'll come and clean my house to find old and unused clothing, shoes, purses, and even furniture to send to her relatives. That's just the way my mom is: she takes care of people she loves.

Changes

Eventually, my mom worked for an airline as well as taking care of my brother and me. During this early part of my childhood, our relationship was good, but I always felt she was harder on me than my brother. I sometimes wonder if this bias came from her Hispanic culture, in which boys often become the apple of their mother's eye, and girls are held to higher standards. But while we were still living with my dad, the preferences balanced out: Mama's boy and Daddy's girl. I didn't feel a void until my father left.

My parents divorced when I was seven. My mother, like my brother, was held to a high standard by my father; he expected perfection and obedience. He, on the other hand, seemed exempt from certain vows. Even before the divorce, I was aware something wasn't quite right. Dad would take me out, and sometimes those field trips would end up at other houses, with other women living in them. I remember one sweet woman who bought me ice cream and gave me other things I wanted. She even made me a doll. I didn't know they were bribes. Dad would always tell me not to say where we'd been, expecting me to keep his secrets. I don't remember all the details of these meetings, but I do remember the ice cream.

And I remember the constant arguing between my parents.

My mother found out about my meetings with Ice Cream Lady when the government sent my father to Egypt for a work project. He'd gotten bold in his disloyalty and had lent Ice Cream Lady his truck. She'd made a copy of his keys, including the one to the house. One day while he was gone, she let herself in, intent on talking to my mom. My mom, of course, was not pleased and yelled at her to leave.

"Please don't hurt her," I cried. "She's my friend!"

The fact that I knew the woman was a breaking point for my mom. She'd been aware of my father's cheating for a while, but my presence at some of those liaisons, and the gifts from one of those women, was too much for her to accept.

The consequences were swift. Stanley Mack, another military man who'd later become my stepfather, swept in and swept her off her feet. Divorce papers greeted my father when he got back to the States.

Sixty days after her divorce was finalized, my mother remarried. It was 1984. We'd moved out of the house but were only a few streets away from my dad. My brother and I spent every other weekend with him. At first, he tried to get custody of me after the divorce, but my mother insisted I stay with her. After we started calling our new stepfather *Daddy*, my biological father, whom I continued to call *Dad*, drifted further away from us—emotionally, if not physically. He was of the opinion that kids only had one mother and one father, and he no longer fit that role in our family.

That was the first time I experienced real grief. My dad was my life. I was his baby girl, his princess, his brat. How could he be so distant to me? I didn't understand. And it broke my heart.

My bond with my mom and brother remained tight. But it took several years for me to get tight with Daddy, my stepfather. Things were immediately a little different living in the house with Daddy. For one, he was more lenient with my brother, and for another, he introduced us to meat. As I mentioned earlier, we had been vegetarians as part of our Seventh-day Adventist practices. Then one day, my brother and I stumbled across Mom slow-roasting ribs for her new husband. We snuck a taste, and it was all over after that. Now, I love meat. My husband and I even own a successful barbeque restaurant, where ribs are featured on the menu.

Savannah

We also had to move around a bit with Daddy, in accordance with the changing tides of military life. Our first move was to Kansas, where my brother and I saw snow for the first time. Then, when I was about eight, when we were still in Kansas, Daddy got deployed to South Korea. Mom went with him and stayed for a few months, and my brother and I went to live in Savannah with Daddy's family for that year.

Daddy's mama was strict! She ran the roost, and spanking was her preferred motivator to get kids to toe the line. She spanked us so much that most of the time we didn't even know what it was for. As much as the word makes me cringe now, we called her Jailer because of all her rules and punishments. Sometimes my brother and I would get so upset we'd call our biological father and tell him about being hit. He'd get mad and tell us he'd come get us, but nothing ever came of that.

But there were light spots too. Behind us was another house where our new best friends lived with their grandmother. She ran a little candy store. Seeing a store completely devoted to candy—and going in it—was a revelation. Now and Later became my favorite.

The outdoors was our playground, even on steamy summer days. The drone of cicadas was ever-present, and Spanish moss trailed from the trees. It always moved slightly, even when there was no obvious breeze. They say Savannah is full of ghosts, so maybe that was it.

It rained a lot, too—sometimes sudden, drenching downpours that would clear the streets as if the Rapture had finally come. We'd play in the rain, even in the winter when it was cold. School wasn't far away and was filled with regular kids instead of military brats. We'd walk there and back. If it was just my brother and me, we'd dawdle on the way home, playing with whatever interesting pieces of nature or people we found. The swamps, especially, held mysteries we were eager to explore. There was always the chance we'd see alligators and crocodiles, those big, ancient-looking beasts that looked to have crawled out of the pages of a fairy tale—one of the scary ones, where the kids get lost in the woods, and the trees close in around them with reaching, bony fingers.

Mom returned from South Korea and lived with us in the house in Savannah instead of finding a place for us to live. It was one of her efforts to save money. But that meant we still had to live with Jailer, who was adamant about keeping to the restrictions of her faith.

As Seventh-day Adventists, we had to stop playing and watching TV from when the sun went down on Friday to when it went down on Saturday. Saturday, according to the Bible, was the seventh day when God rested and deemed a rest day by the Ten Commandments. So we rested. A twenty-four-hour fast from childish distractions. We hated it since the good cartoons always aired on Saturday mornings. Despite our dislike, this conditioning stuck because when I started sneaking out of the house as a teenager, I'd only sneak out on Saturday nights. Of course, Saturday night was when all the good parties would be.

Maybe Savannah was another kind of fast, a moment out of time. The city certainly felt as if it was frozen in place. The oppressive heat and humidity that lays on you like a heavy quilt may have had something to do with that, or all the old buildings, or the echoes of a history filled with pain and grief. For me, it was a slowing down, a respite of sorts before the next phase of my life, when things would speed up.

New Family

When we returned to El Paso, we discovered our biological father had someone new to introduce to us: a woman he intended to marry. Tony and I were in their wedding party, but that didn't mean we had an easy relationship with the woman.

They lived on the same military base we did. We were so close; it was only a five- or six-minute walk to visit our dad and this bobcat he had as a pet...and his new wife. It was so hard for me to accept her. Yes, my dad had already started to distance himself from me and my brother by that point, but I still had hope in my little-girl heart that he'd want me back in his life one day. Now that he was married, it felt like someone had permanently taken my place. Someone who had a different lifestyle and different expectations of me.

She was a nice lady who tried to dress me like a Barbie doll and put flowers in my hair, which I probably would have loved if my mom had done it. But this woman did it in a way that made me feel like I wasn't good enough as-is. She made me feel like I wasn't living up to her expectations. It got to a point where I gave her a little attitude and tried to avoid her, which didn't go over well with my father, who was all about rules and respect.

He insisted Tony and I call her "auntie" because we already had a mom. He demanded we respect her and do as she wished. His siding with her felt like another slice through the thin cord that now connected us and dashed any hope I had of ever reclaiming that special place in his heart.

Seeing Differences

I was ten years old when we returned to El Paso, and I began attending middle school the following fall. I was a straight-A student, still caring about the report card I no longer got rewarded for. My best friend was Tamika. We were in a little dance group together, and we'd have sleepovers at each other's houses on the weekends. But the carelessness of childhood wouldn't last much longer.

Simple camping trips to the park in Ruidoso, New Mexico, just on the other side of the Texas border, became trips to visit my aunt and her son. *Tía* Amanda was amazing and so much fun—until she got mad. If she was mad, you'd better run because she'd hit you with whatever was closest: a fly swatter, a shoe, whatever.

When I was eleven, *tía* Amanda started taking me to *quinceañeras*, those beautiful and lavish parties thrown for Hispanic girls when they turn fifteen to celebrate coming into womanhood. Suddenly, I became aware of the wondrous world of glamorous things that I'd been missing under my mother's austere watch. She had insisted we couldn't afford the time and expense of going to these big parties. At the time, she was in the middle of her schooling, a schooling she took seriously because, while she could afford it with the financial assistance of Daddy, she knew she couldn't depend on that security forever. Men could come and go, as she'd found. So she thought it was her responsibility to get ahead while she could, to hedge her bets in case she needed to be our sole provider in the future.

Kids, however, don't understand this kind of adulting. Nor can they see the dangers and long-term consequences of their behavior. I began growing up fast, perhaps too fast, and I started comparing my life to the lives of other girls my age. As I did, the distance and differences between my mom and me that had simmered since early childhood rose to the forefront.

Northeast El Paso is a military town. Fort Bliss is one of the biggest army bases in the country, so most of the mix of white and Hispanic kids at my school were army kids. The west side of town where we lived was a suburb of retirees and a sprinkling of young families that had chosen to make El Paso home after the constant movement from base to base. This more stable environment included my family—my well-organized family.

Mom wielded rules and schedules like a weapon against unseen forces of evil influence. Influences like my cousin Julie, whom I thought of as a sister and idolized because, in her lawless household, she got to do anything, go anywhere, and meet anybody, and she had so much fun. Meanwhile, for me, there was a schedule I had to follow from the time I got up to the time I went to bed. It was posted on my bedroom door: this is when you watch TV; this is when you read; this is when you eat. We only had one small TV in the living room.

My brother and I had to take turns picking out the cartoons we wanted to see, while constantly under the watchful eye of our mother.

She seemed to be cut from the same practical military cloth she'd been surrounded by much of her life. She was a servant and a nurturer, but also a get-it-as-you-need-it kind of person. When my brother and I would ask for the same things we saw our friends getting—requests that skyrocketed as we became teenagers—she'd come back with a quick and firm no. To her, "We can't afford that," translated to "You don't need that."

Christmas wasn't on one particular day in our household; it was supposed to be all year long, but while that sounds fantastic as an idea, it never translated to more gifts. I especially couldn't understand that mindset. It made no sense to me. I was old enough to know that Daddy was a sergeant major in the military and that money wasn't an issue because my mom received child support from my dad. Every time she'd say no to me, I'd go ask my dad, and he'd say, "No. I pay child support."

Our new daddy was a bit soft with the money, though—if we caught him on a good day. He'd check to see if we'd asked Mom first. Even if we had and she'd said no, he'd usually cave, especially if we caught him shortly after he came home from a stint in the field. He oversaw tankers and had to leave the base for long stretches at a time. When he'd return, it was like hitting the jackpot. He'd give us whatever we wanted.

Still, he wasn't always home, and meanwhile, our friends, whose lower-ranking fathers made less, seemed to afford stuff just fine, even with only one parent working.

Why shouldn't we have the nice things our friends did? I didn't understand, and I felt cheated. To top it off, I was too young to work, so I couldn't even earn my own pocket money. I was ripe for an alternative way of getting the things I thought I needed to fit in.

Fitting in was important to me. I wasn't popular in school. My faith made me a little different. I couldn't wear makeup like all the other girls my age. And although I was biracial, I looked Black, with my fuller lips and kinkier hair, and there weren't many other Black girls among the Hispanics and white kids at my school. The other kids would call me Big Lips. They'd call me nigger and make fun of my kinky hair. They'd call me ugly. At twelve, thirteen, and fourteen, when your life revolves around friends and social status, those heavy words load up on you. They become a burden. My self-esteem tanked, and I thought no one would ever love me, would ever accept me as worthy of being around them.

That longing for acceptance cut deep within me. Looking back, I can now see why. I felt I'd been shoved out of my father's life. I felt like an outsider among my peers. All I wanted was to be accepted, to feel as if I were a wanted part of a larger whole.

Though the desire was strong in me, I know I'm not the only one who ever struggled to find a place where she belonged. It happens a lot, especially with young girls. We just want to be accepted by others. We want it so bad, we start doing things, experimenting, to see if we can find our way into a larger whole. Whatever we do that gets rewarded by others letting us into their circles, we repeat. And repeat. And repeat. Until we carry those new behaviors into adulthood, not really understanding they aren't part of who we truly are. By then, the rewards aren't apparent, and the consequences can be traumatic.

I found a way to be accepted by becoming a people pleaser. It started off innocently enough: I'd buy snacks for others at lunch. It grew to me lying, saying things to make people think I was just like them or somehow more likable.

Things worsened when my parents bought that house off-base. I started drinking so I could fit in with the cool kids in my Hispanic neighborhood when I was about twelve or thirteen. I tried to dance like them and listen to country music because that was what they listened to. It wasn't the music my dad had introduced me to—it wasn't the music I loved—but I pretended I was all in.

Things only ramped up from there. I found myself ganging up on other girls as I went through an initiation period of sorts. My "friends" would say, "Go pull that girl's hair," or tell me to be mean to someone to prove that I was "good enough" to hang with them. I'd do it. I did whatever they wanted if that meant I'd be accepted by them.

The power of peer pressure on kids is immense. You measure yourself by the yardstick of your friends—what they do, what they have, what they look like. You want their life, the one you see from the outside and imagine is perfect on the inside. But that life doesn't exist. It never exists. And you're left reaching for nothing but fluff and air. You'd think as more jaded adults we'd get over these fantasies, but many of us still prefer the dream over the reality. We keep our own painful stories secret and project only the life we want others to see. I have many friends on Instagram and Facebook who think my life is glamorous and that nothing ever goes wrong, but I paid for that normalcy many times with my own blood and tears. Those payments began when I was in middle school.

I learned some of my friends in El Paso snuck out at night to go to parties. That sounded so exciting and glamorous. I wanted to go too. But how? My mom wouldn't let me do that. Besides, what would I wear? Mom always cautious about money, refusing to fund the clothes and accessories that fit the party-girl lifestyle.

One day, I told Karina, an older and more experienced party girl, that I liked her new shoes. She was quick to tell me how she got them. "My boyfriend bought me these."

"What?" I was amazed. Such a method of procurement had never occurred to me. I'd always thought the only two options for getting spending money were your parents or a job.

"Yeah, girl. You just need to come and hang out with us. Sneak out. Meet guys. Lie about your age. You'll get tons of stuff," she assured me.

It sounded like a sweet deal. And not too far off from my prior experience with adult men. My mother may have held her ground with money, but I had found, both with my dad and my daddy, that I could eventually get what I wanted from them. Manipulating other men just seemed like a natural progression of that skill.

Boys

My first boyfriend, my first love, Daniel, was a Crip, a member of the Oldies but Goodies family. Like the name suggests, they'd hang out in Ascarate Park—and I'd hang out with them—drinking Mad Dog 20/20 or Boone's Farm, grilling meats, smoking weed, and listening to the oldies but goodies music. Some of the music was the same that my dad had introduced me to, but there was also some rock and roll. Everything from "I'm Your Puppet" by James & Bobby Purify to "Stairway to Heaven" by the O'Jays. I loved it all. I felt like I'd finally found someplace where I belonged.

I was able to identify with the music, with the words and the sound. I'd go out cruising with Daniel the way I used to with my dad, only in a cool car: a low-rider decked out with fancy rims and everything. So, yes, I wanted to be accepted so badly that I wound up hanging out with the Crips. They sold weed around me, which wasn't legal at the time. And there was ecstasy, which we'd take while listening to Pink Floyd.

We'd play spades in the park, make a lot of noise back-talking each other in fun, laughing. If someone called and said, "Hey, I'm coming over, so start grilling," other people would show up with more food. If someone called and said, "I'm having issues with so-and-so," that meant everybody had an issue with so-and-so. We were like a family—a family with drugs and guns. But I wasn't scared. They were my protectors. I was accepted.

Of course, I had to sneak out of the house to catch the bus to go see Daniel. At fourteen, that wasn't always the easiest thing to do. Sometimes, my mom would find out. "Over my dead body will you go see him!" she'd yell.

"You'd better move!" I'd yell back and go anyway. Or I'd sneak out my bedroom window at night. She'd either like it, or she wouldn't, and I told myself I didn't care. Of course, she never liked it. More than once I'd return and fight with her about it, sometimes with fists.

It's interesting to look back. I realize now that I was playing the part my mother might have expected me to play. Back-talking and rebelling against your parents was normal in the Hispanic community I was in. I thought this was how you were supposed to act as a daughter. Even as a girlfriend, I was doing what I'd seen around me: tolerating poor or even illegal behavior by boyfriends because they were good to me. These were the relationships you were supposed to have. I didn't know anything different. The friends I admired, my role models, were all doing the same. If this was how life was supposed to go, what could go wrong?

Granted, my mom did attempt to counteract these influences. Family, education, and thankfulness were values set down by our religion. We'd always have house chores. It had to be spotless before we could go out and play. She taught us to cook, especially me, since cooking was an important skill to have as a wife and mother. But education, as with my biological father, was her golden ticket to a better life.

She'd enrolled as a student at three different local community colleges to work toward her bachelor's degree when we moved back to El Paso. She'd take classes while we were in school and be home in the afternoons. She made sure we had breakfast every morning, a home-cooked meal every night, and a clean house. She asked about our day and helped us with homework. But her books never left the dining table until the end of the semester, and we ate dinner in the living room. She was also still working for an airline. All told, being a mom, student, and worker gave us no time to socialize as a family or with family friends. My mother told me much later that she worried about this lack.

As I said, education was very important to her, and her dream for us was a college degree. She thought her efforts to get a teaching degree, then her graduate degree at the University of Texas at El

Paso, would be a good example for us. Perhaps, to some extent, it was, because I maintained good grades even as other aspects of my behavior slipped. While the dining table was off-limits to dinner, I'd always find a space to do my homework. I don't remember ever *not* being a good student. My brother would play outside in his treehouse, and I would study. I've kept this studiousness into adulthood.

Who's to say whether all the pulls on her attention contributed to my rebellion or whether the stones in that path had been slowly set throughout my childhood and I was now locked into my fate? Only in hindsight can we start to make sense of it all, pick apart the pieces to find out how everything fits together. I'm still not entirely sure why I did what I did—teenage brains are a mystery, even when they are your own.

All I know is God allowed me to live through it, beginning with what happened next.

Chapter 2
Child Bride

As I improved my ability to sneak out of the house, my friend Karina found more parties for us to attend. One Saturday night, when I was just fourteen years old, I wound up at a frat party at nearby New Mexico State University in Las Cruces. There, I met someone new. A tall, dark, handsome man named Horace.

Horace flashed a lot of money around, bought me food, and called me gorgeous. Perhaps obviously, he was older, twenty-two, in fact, and had the mature body to go with it. He stood six foot two, had smooth chocolate skin, and was stacked. He fulfilled all my teenage romance fantasies, and I was more than flattered by his attention.

I told Horace I was eighteen, lying about my age as Karina had advised. I know some fourteen-year-olds legitimately look like they're eighteen, but when I go back to photos from this time, I look like a baby. He had to have known I wasn't telling the truth.

We started dating immediately, and my real age became known, but he didn't care.

I was too young for a driver's license, so he'd pick me up from middle school in his white Oldsmobile Cutlass. That was a car that turned heads. It had a loud stereo system, chrome rims, and a blue velvet interior. I felt so important getting picked up in such a nice car and being whisked into an adult world outside of school and away from my house.

We'd go to the movies. We'd go out to eat, though sometimes we'd stay in and cook together too. He'd take me to his friend's house to play spades. And my favorite: he'd take me shopping. We'd go to stores, and he'd tell me to buy whatever I wanted.

I was awestruck even though my friends thought I was crazy. Especially Daniel, but I didn't pay him any mind. While I considered Daniel the love of my life, I knew I wasn't the love of his life. He had affection toward me, but he was a player. He had a number of other girls at the ready. I never thought I was pretty enough to be his only one; meanwhile, Horace told me I was beautiful.

Daniel knew of Horace outside of me. They were in the same drug-dealing circles, and Daniel had heard things on the streets about him. He wanted me to play it cautious with him. "Don't do it," he said. "Don't be with him. Something isn't good here."

I thought his concern, like that of my other friends, was with our age difference. I dismissed his words. Besides, Daniel was a drug dealer, so who was he to moralize me?

My new knight in shining armor seemed to understand my longing for possessions and praise, much more than my parents did. When a guy tells you you're beautiful while everyone else says you're ugly, and he follows it up with the gifts your parents deny you, the combination is irresistible to a troubled child. So irresistible that I didn't mind the risks involved with sneaking the new clothes he bought me into the house.

"Where did you get that?" my mom would ask.

"Oh, it's Julie's. She left it here and said I could have it." Or "It's Karina's. I borrowed it."

It was a power play for me—getting by with something in front of my mother. My amazing boyfriend gave me something she wouldn't. I'd wear the clothes in front of her, and she never knew the truth. Perhaps that was the first dividing line Horace carved to separate me from my family.

I started to grow apart from my school friends, too, as he seemed to want to spend more and more time with me. I didn't think there was anything wrong with a twenty-two-year-old man paying attention to me. From his money to his praise, all I could focus on were his affirmations that I was worthy and desirable. I began to think he was *it*, the one for me, and we would live happily ever after.

Unintended Parental Influence

Because we *were* spending so much time together, he eventually had to meet my parents. At first, I introduced Horace to them as a friend, not a romantic partner. He was well-spoken and nice. He told my parents he was a student and played basketball at NMSU, which was true at the time. He was also a member of a fraternity. Sure, he was a bit older, but he was supposed to be a respectable college student, and my mom did value education, so she liked him at first too.

He was also a type 1 diabetic and needed sympathy and support for this horrible disease, as he described it to me. I had no idea what diabetes was, really. I took his word and didn't try to research it. I thought he was dying and needed me to make his last days better.

At first, my parents saw him as a good person with good prospects. Everybody did. Horace was an expert at laying on the charm and telling people only what they wanted to hear.

When my mom found out we were actually dating, the tone shifted. She called him a pedophile, among other harsh names. She would flat-out tell me, "You're not going out with him."

I did anyway.

My arguments for my choice were many. I felt important with Horace, for one, valued in a way that I didn't feel at home—I wanted to help him have a better life while he could. He told me he wouldn't live long. I saw him give himself shots of insulin in the leg every day and comment that he just wanted a good life for the time he had left. I wanted to make him happy and help give him that good life.

My mom was sympathetic to his condition but still refused to allow me to see him. So I resorted to threatening her, saying I'd leave home for good if she didn't let me. Or I'd simply disobey and walk out the door to be with him. She treated me like a child, and I didn't feel like a child, especially when I was with Horace. He made me feel like the woman all teenage girls aspire to be: a woman who didn't need her mother telling her what to do.

But my mom knew the price of growing up too soon. Unplanned pregnancy, especially one outside of marriage, among other dangers, made her sick with worry. When trying to control me with her rules failed, she turned to higher-level rules. On one particular night, a few months into our relationship, she threatened to accuse him of statutory rape if I didn't stop seeing him. It was the only card she had left to play. But my mom's forbidding negativity only made me crave his sympathetic presence more. After rushing to his side, I told him her ultimatum, the latest in a string of complaints about her obstructions to our relationship. He made me an offer I didn't want to refuse: "Why don't we just get married?"

My fate was sealed just as glibly as his offer was made. "Sure, let's do it!"

That was when my age became an issue. I was too young to sign the papers on my own and needed my parents' permission to marry. The fight between my mother and me over that consent was epic.

"I didn't raise you to do this!" she yelled. I thought my mom's words were slightly hypocritical since she'd married young and had sisters who married at an even younger age. If they could, why couldn't I?

"You are supposed to get your diploma! Go to college!" Those were her words, but I interpreted her as saying, *Go ahead and ruin your life.* It was just one more disapproval in a line of so many that only made me more determined.

So I gave my mother an ultimatum: accept my choice of husband or never see me again. She relented. I guess the fear of losing me for good, after the constant arguments and running away, was real.

In fairness to my mom, there was also a cultural component to her consent. Marrying young was common for her family. Many of my cousins got married at the age of fifteen, some as young as fourteen, and her extended family didn't think the age difference was such a big deal when she consulted with her mother and sisters about it, even though my mother felt it was wrong.

Or maybe she was just too tired to say no any longer. I was at the height of my rebellion. In addition to sneaking out, I'd tried to become a stripper to go work with my cousin, a plan my mom had flatly refused. And once, when she told me to wash the dishes, I retorted, "I'll wash the dishes," and broke them all on the floor. I was willful and determined to resist her. Not only that, but I threatened to run away so I could be with Horace and promised she would never see me again. One of my mom's biggest fears was losing me completely, so perhaps the thought of allowing me to marry a man she didn't like was better than risking losing me for forever.

Whatever the case, after that last argument, everything just fell into place. I met his mother in New Mexico, and though she questioned my age, she gave in to our desires. I'd won. I got my man. I was the only eighth grader who was engaged. I destroyed chances of going to homecoming or a prom, but why should I need those childhood milestones when I only needed my new love?

The Wedding

At fifteen, Mexican girls celebrate coming into womanhood with a *quinceañera*. They get decked out in a grand dress, and their parents throw a grand party.

Instead of a *quinceañera*, I had a black-and-white wedding.

We had the dress made in Juarez, El Paso's Mexican sister city right across the border. It was big and ornate, a true princess dress that required several trips to the seamstress for alterations. I had two bridesmaids in black-and-white dresses, also made in Mexico, and two groomsmen in tuxedos, and I had a flower girl and ring bearer.

My hair was perfect. My makeup was on point. My dress fit like a dream. I was everything I wanted to be, and I was about to have a fairy-tale wedding: a beautiful princess about to marry her prince.

Not everyone saw it that way.

My dad, my biological father, met me at the church. I walked inside and found him waiting for me. "Let's talk," is how he greeted me.

We headed down a hall toward the restrooms. I was expecting a loving father-daughter conversation. He'd tell me I was beautiful and that he was proud of me. Instead, he stopped by the water fountains, turned toward me, and made me face him directly. "This is all wrong," he said. "Don't do it."

"What do you mean?" I stared into his dark brown eyes, unable to process that he wasn't giving me his blessing.

"Don't marry that man." His face was stern, not proud. "You don't have to do this."

"But I want to! I love him!"

"I will give you ten thousand dollars. Look," he pulled a check out of his pocket. "Walk out of this church with me right now, and the money is all yours."

I couldn't believe my father wasn't supporting me. Because I was so young, my mom had to sign papers allowing me to get married. My dad didn't want anything to do with it when I first told him, but I felt certain he'd change his mind. Why wouldn't he? I was so happy!

But no. I was in the middle of a dream come true—*my* dream come true. There was a handsome prince waiting for me at the end of the aisle in the next room. I wanted to be with him. A man who had a disease that could kill him. He needed me, wanted me—me!— as his wife to help him have a good life with what little time he had left. Why couldn't my father understand that?

"Listen," Dad continued, "you don't have to do this. I'll send you to Rhode Island to live with my family for a few months. You can rebuild your life and come back and—"

"No! I love him! I want to marry him!"

And I did.

I actually walked down the aisle, arm-in-arm with my dad, even though he disagreed, even though he thought it was statutory rape, that it wasn't normal, and that it wasn't right. He did it to support me. He led me to the altar where my maid of honor and bridesmaids were waiting for me, as was Horace, my prince, standing with his groomsmen, friends of his from college.

It was the greatest day of my life—there I was, the center of everyone's attention with this charming man who became my husband. Standing in his church—now *our* church—I promised to love, cherish, and obey him all my life, 'til death do us part, and he promised me the same thing. Afterward, we had a celebratory buffet dinner at a swanky Chinese restaurant Mom and Daddy had rented. All evening long, I was special; I was beautiful; I was everything I wanted to be.

Horace and me, after saying our vows.

My dad helping me into the limo.

Horace and my maid of honor.

My little brother, LC, and me at the reception.

Me with my groom.

But my father was right: it was all wrong. Of course, I was deaf to rational thought at the time. Maybe we all were. My mom had convinced herself and my daddy that my marrying a twenty-two-year-old man was for the best. Horace's parents accepted it. His stepdad was his best man! Our extended family and friends all accepted it. Even Horace's groomsmen, who were his college basketball buddies. They had laughed about our wedding, needled him when they first heard about it. "Man! She's only fifteen! She's not even developed yet!" But they ate the catered Chinese food and danced to the music with my cousins and friends like it was all good with them.

With the lone exception of my biological father, we were all happy that night, which should have been impossible, considering that my relationship with my new husband had started when I met him only about six months prior.

Unless you've actually been in a similar situation, you probably cannot understand what would lead a girl—by her own choice—to fight so fiercely to marry a man almost ten years her senior. Honestly, I don't quite understand it at this point either, except to say that in my immature mind, I couldn't fathom that a good-looking man, one who gave me the lifestyle I wanted and who constantly showered me with the attention I craved, would turn out to be a monster. I was still young enough to believe fairy-tale happy endings could come true in real life, that a handsome prince could rescue me. He would help me escape the negative way my peers saw me and the controlling nature of my home life.

But the life I thought he would give me truly was a fantasy that slowly dissolved into horror the longer I was with him.

Honeymoon, Interrupted

There was no honeymoon after our wedding. My dream life with Horace didn't fare much better. In fact, it lasted fewer than twenty-four hours.

We got married on a Saturday. By Sunday, Horace and I moved into what would be our home: his parents' place in New Mexico. I lost my virginity that night. When I got up the next morning, we all went to church, and when we returned, I discovered my days of being a princess were officially over.

"Make me breakfast," my mother-in-law, Lorraine, ordered me. "I want eggs."

I wanted to tell her to make her own damn eggs, but all I could get out was, "I'm not cooking."

"Yes, you are," she told me. "That's what you're supposed to be doing. You have duties now as a wife. It says so in the Bible. You're supposed to serve your husband and his family. You're supposed to be our hands and feet. Now, I want eggs."

So I made her eggs. I cleaned up after her, too. That night, I made the whole family dinner and, yes, cleaned up after them all. Instead of going to school the next day, I served my husband and his family. I did their laundry, cleaned their house, and cooked their meals. Somehow, I was living the reverse situation of what happened to Cinderella—I went from being a beautiful princess bride to being a servant in the ashes. In more ways than one.

I knew my new husband was a drug dealer. I knew that was how he made all his money. Even before we were married, I knew that was what he did, as I'd even seen him and his stepdad, Ted, selling out of the Cutlass. But Daniel had sold dope, too, and I thought he was a good person. My closest friends were gang bangers and drug dealers. So the correlation between drugs and danger was lost on me.

Daddy was of a different mindset. He suspected drugs were in the mix, but after a conversation with him before we got married, Horace took a job as a cook at the Village Inn, so it looked like he came by his money honestly. I fooled myself into believing the drugs were just a small side hustle. The extent and ramifications of his trade didn't hit me until I moved in with Horace and his parents.

I became an accomplice after the fact for the first time within a week of becoming a wife. After a couple of days of playing maid for my husband's family, I saw Ted, my new father-in-law, smoking something in a pipe. Soon, he said he was numb. I asked Horace what was going on, and that was when he showed me how he made crack on the kitchen stove. And then he told me to clean up the mess he'd just made cooking it. This would hardly be my last experience with drugs, their paraphernalia, and their mess. Frequently, when Lorraine was at work, Horace and Ted would have crack parties, and I'd have to deal with the aftermath. And then there were all the needles Lorraine would bring home from her job as a nurse that Ted would take for his own drug use.

It didn't take long for me to realize I'd gone straight from one set of shackles to another. My mom had put me on a tight schedule with rigorous study demands. Now, I was put to work. The shock of it all made me pliable—this was what I signed up for as a wife, right? This was what God wanted me to do...but I couldn't help feeling that my new family's God was more demanding than the God of my not-so-distant childhood.

Changing Faiths

As a Seventh-day Adventist, Horace's church, a Pentecostal one, took some getting used to. Three months before the wedding, I started attending his church with him. I thought this was another sign of our compatibility. We were doing things together. It was sweet and only made me love him more.

Though we were both Christian, the two denominations were like apples and oranges. As Pentecostals, we were in church all the time—Tuesdays, Fridays, Saturdays, and Sundays. Mostly, the congregation was Black women during the week. Seemed like their husbands only showed up on Sundays. My mother didn't understand why I was OK going to that church. She was bewildered by the speaking in tongues, the ecstatic dancing and singing, the miraculous professions from the pulpit. She had never seen anything like that in the Catholic churches of her youth or the Seventh-day Adventist one.

I thought this way of praising God was all very exciting compared with the more formal gatherings of my family's church, but even though I was willing to move away from my family and friends, it was hard to move away from the church of my youth, especially to one so strange.

Admittedly, the speaking in tongues thing bewildered me too. It just sounded like a bunch of gibberish, with everyone flinging themselves around and talking at no one. They explained this was the language the disciples spoke when the Holy Ghost went into them. It was holy speech. "You're not Christian until you speak in tongues!" they'd admonish me. "We're gonna pray it into you!" They'd take me up to the altar, pour holy oil on me, and press my head down. Someone looking at this from the outside might've seen it as a bizarre form of water torture. It didn't force the Holy Spirit into me, but it did force me to speak in tongues—or at least fake it. I just wanted them to stop. Years down the line, after many more hours in church and reading the Bible for myself, I would feel the urge to speak in tongues, but it wasn't often.

Eventually, I got used to all the strangeness. My husband and his family were my new norm, and I was willing to change to please them. Their church became the center of my world, and they used it to control me. At the time, my mother called their ways crazy. Later, we'd both call it brainwashing.

The church helped solidify in me the belief that wives were supposed to leave their families and go live with their husbands' families to serve them, which translated to maid duties. Lorraine, as a nurse and the sole honest provider for the household, was gone a lot, and the men certainly weren't going to do domestic chores. So I cooked, cleaned, washed, and acted as caregiver. I was now thankful

Horace had no siblings so I only had to pick up after the three of them.

I was expected to have all the chores done and dinner on the table when Lorraine and Horace got home. I made everybody else's plate up first. I ate last. I could have sported heels and a dress like those wives from 1950s sitcoms, especially since I was now forbidden to wear pants. However, I was also forbidden to wear makeup, and my hair was always in a ponytail. That was what Lorraine had advised me to do. She told me it was a sacrifice I had to make.

My mom was horrified when I told her how I lived. "That's not right!" she'd exclaim, incensed on my behalf. "That's not the way of the Bible! They're manipulating you. You can't even see it. You're a slave!"

It probably isn't a surprise that Horace and his family no longer wanted me visiting or even talking to my mom. For a while, they forbade me to see her or any other member of my family. They wanted to separate me from my prior life and relationships. Isolate me and make me depend on them in all ways—at first, I didn't have a paying job (and couldn't even get one at fifteen), so all trips away from the house needed their blessing and their cash.

It wouldn't be until Horace started hitting me that I thought to move back home. But before that happened, Junior came into the picture.

Sacrifice

Being a full-time housewife meant I had no time for school. I wound up dropping out of school early in ninth grade but not because I moved in with my in-laws, and not because of my household duties, which did strain my educational aspirations quite a bit. I quit school because I got pregnant. Nine months after my wedding day, shortly after I turned sixteen, I became a mom.

My mother, being a dutiful Christian, hadn't given me "the talk" about where babies came from before my marriage. I had no idea birth control even existed—not that Horace or his parents would have let me use it. Their faith demanded "be fruitful and multiply," and that was what they did.

Sex was an obligation, a duty to be performed by the wife in order to have kids. Horace wasn't a help here. He didn't explain anything about how sex or my body worked. I was told to lie there, that it wasn't going to hurt. I was his wife now, and I was supposed to do whatever he told me to do. I didn't know then that many would call this rape.

Chapter 3
In the Devil's Den

I don't remember the first time Horace hit me.

Not only do I not remember the first time I was hit, but I don't remember why I "earned" that punishment. Maybe it was because I didn't have the house clean enough or the food done on time. I do remember fighting about those things a lot. Other times it was because I said I didn't want to have sex with him. Or because Daniel, my old boyfriend, contacted me.

Daniel would check in on me every now and then to make sure I was doing OK. Sometimes, if a fight with Horace got bad enough, I'd tell Daniel about it. Those conversations simultaneously scared me and solaced me. More than once, Daniel would say, "I don't wanna have to kill Horace, but if things don't settle down, I will." I knew he meant it. And I knew the Oldies but Goodies family could load up and do a drive-by shooting if they felt it was necessary. I didn't want that to be necessary.

It's ironic that, in my desire to write this book, I now have to remember the things I've tried my best to forget. While I don't remember the first time he hit me, I do remember the first time I landed in the hospital because of his beatings. I was still pregnant with Junior.

I found myself surrounded by nurses and doctors in the ER who wanted to know what had happened. I told them I fell down the stairs. (That became my usual line during hospital trips. It was the only accident I could think of that would explain the broken bones and multiple bruises.)

The nurses in their blue scrubs seemed scared for me. They easily saw through my lies and told me I should leave him. "What are you even doing there?" they asked. "Why are you even married? What are you doing married? You're so young!" I'd come to hear those lines too many times. Always, they'd ask, *What are you doing married?* And then follow it up with, *You are so young!*

I never had answers to their questions. And once, when a white nurse gave me a domestic abuse hotline number to call, I knew I wouldn't know how to answer their questions either, so I threw the number away. The Bible said I had to stand by my man. I held onto the cold comfort of the twisted web of religion my new family had woven for me: I had to leave my father and mother and cleave to my husband. Love him like Christ loved the church, a love that included trial and sacrifice.

By the time of that first trip to the ER, Horace had sufficiently separated me from my parents. I thought I had no family to go back to. But either the ER doctors were convincing enough or my love for my family ran deeper than my fear of Horace because I wound up calling them from the hospital, now pregnant, bruised, and beaten.

They wanted me to come back home, begged me to. I went that first time. The nurses released me to my parents. They took me to their home, but I was only there a short while. It didn't take long for Horace to come claim me. He and my stepdad had some words that day.

"You're what? Six two? Six three?" my daddy, my shield, asked. "You're a big guy. You have no business hitting my daughter. You wanna hit somebody, hit me."

My parents wanted me to stay with them, but Horace's hold was too strong. So I returned to my "prince," and life went on as before, just the same, except I knew my parents still loved me.

Eventually, I realized there was a pattern in Horace's behavior. First would come the verbal abuse. He'd yell at me, accuse me of not being a good wife, of not following God's commands. Those were my sins. If he wasn't placated after the verbal assaults, then the physical ones would start. My penance would be in the form of beatings.

Humans are remarkable. They can get used to a lot of things, and no matter how bad those things are, if you can predict them, there's a sort of safety in that. And as is so common in abusive relationships, the devil you know, no matter how evil, seems better than the devil you don't. For a young woman with no job, money, or friends, and eventually with young children in tow, that unknown devil is very scary.

When I gave birth to my first child, still a child myself, I begged Horace to let me see my mom and introduce her to her first grandchild. He refused. The day after I came home from the hospital, I had to cook for everyone on top of taking sole care of my newborn. It hurt. I didn't heal very quickly, physically or emotionally. But by this time, I didn't have much protest left in me, and postpartum depression was a luxury I couldn't afford.

Abusing the Kids

Horace didn't turn violent against his kids until our second child, Kenneth, was born—a year after Junior.

Granted, with Junior, he was still very strict. As a baby, when Junior cried, he wouldn't let me go pick him up. My three-month-old would scream at the top of his lungs, but Horace dismissed his distress. "He'll live. Don't make him a sissy. He don't need you."

Junior avoided the worst of Horace's anger, probably because he looked just like his daddy, even as a baby. Horace was happy about that and would act the proud poppa most of the time with him.

Kenneth didn't look like his daddy. He came out lighter in color. And Horace resented him and me for some sort of perceived unfaithfulness, and this anger only grew over time.

When I said Kenneth was born a year after Junior, I meant an exact year. They have the same birthday. The doctors had advised me to abstain from sex for six weeks after Junior's birth, but Horace resented anyone telling him what to do with his wife. In between cooking, cleaning, and childcare, I'd be ordered to lay with my husband. My body was exhausted; my spirit was crushed. Horace still refused to let my mother see or visit me.

Me & Kenneth

I wanted to see my parents. I ached for my mother to help me. I remembered the conversation my stepfather had with Horace and knew my parents would take me back. I got brave enough to go see my mom a few times and began to talk, in earnest, about going home for good and taking my tiny sons with me. That only ramped up Horace's demands. "You're not going anywhere," he'd tell me. "You're gonna cook. You're gonna clean. And you're gonna lay with me, or I'm gonna kill everybody in your family."

So I learned how to be a mom on my own, as Lorraine didn't feel it was her responsibility to advise me.

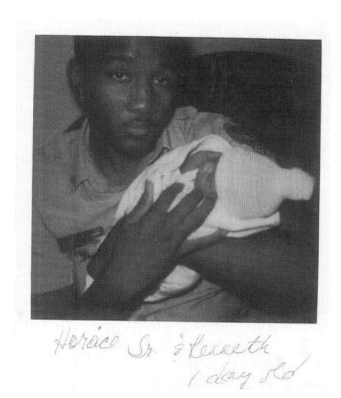

Horace Sr. & Kenneth
1 day old

Another Trip to the ER

A second trip to the ER, this time with both my boys in tow, started our case with Child Protective Services (CPS).

The El Paso hospital was a mandatory reporter, which means if they suspected child abuse, they had to report it. On that trip, they

45

did both. I can't help but wonder why a sixteen-year-old was never considered a child in their eyes. I'd been there so many times before, had a file filled with all sorts of injuries caused by "falling down the stairs." Nurse after nurse would shake their head as they wrote down the flimsy excuse, but no one ever thought to call CPS until one day when I came in pretty beaten up and pregnant again. I had no one else who could watch the babies, so I took them with me.

Kenneth, at two weeks old, happened to be running a fever that day. The nurses took him away from me to examine him. Shortly after, a skinny white lady wearing big glasses showed up. She came at me directly. "This is not normal. This is abuse. You'll need to take parenting classes and change your ways, or we're going to take your kids." She then called my parents, as I refused to do it myself.

This was the first time I'd seen my mother in months. "Look what Horace did to my child!" I sobbed to my mother. She turned Kenneth's little barefoot over to discover, to her horror, small circular burns on the bottoms of her grandson's feet. They matched the burns on his belly, where Horace had burnt off the remains of his umbilical cord, leading to an infection and his fever. Horace had been putting his cigarettes and joints out on his two-week-old son, in places not immediately noticeable.

"He did this?" she hissed.

"Yes."

She immediately alerted my daddy. Both now upset, they demanded a change: "You're not going back to him. You're going to stay with us. We will help you through this."

But I couldn't. Horace and I had recently moved into our own place. We had a townhome—just him, me, and the kids. There was no way he was going to let me move back in with my family. He had me to himself in that townhome, where he wanted me to be.

"Don't go back," the CPS worker said. "You're young. You have your whole life and your family's support. You need to leave." I was terrified to listen to them—what would Horace do? Besides, the Bible said I had to cleave to my husband.

The CPS worker also tried to threaten me in the hopes I'd come to my senses. "If you go back," it was promised, "we'll take your kids and put you in jail for child abuse."

But I couldn't leave Horace.

They felt sorry for me. I was under eighteen, in the hospital with my abused two-week-old son, my one-year-old on my lap, and already pregnant again with my third child. Their sympathy probably kept me out of jail at that time.

Because CPS preferred to keep kids with their parents if at all possible, they agreed to allow Horace, me, and the boys to live with my parents for a while. I think they could tell I was brainwashed and hoped my mom would get through to me if I lived with her.

At first, it was so good being back in my parents' home. I was able to heal, finally, from giving birth to Kenneth. I was able to recharge and breathe. My mom did most of the cooking and cleaning. She'd help with the kids. "You just had a baby! Rest!" she'd say. But all her efforts were in vain. Horace kept a watchful eye on me and made sure he still had control of me, something he enforced all too frequently behind closed doors.

To her credit, my mom did her best to chip away at Horace's control. She made me question his decisions and how we were parenting. One day she asked me why we thought it was a good idea to keep an infant and one-year-old out until midnight to attend church services. She had a good point. My babies were exhausted. I knew they needed more sleep.

Horace, of course, didn't even consider what the babies needed.

"I'm still the head of our household!" he yelled. "I'm still your leader!" Then a fight between us ensued, and my parents witnessed it. Horace broke my jaw (or was it my arm that time?) and my daddy pulled a gun on him.

"Listen, I will kill you if you mess with my daughter, again," he threatened.

Horace backed down, temporarily. But it wasn't the only time they were in each other's faces. More than once Daddy physically tried to fight Horace. So did my brother, Tony. Pregnant me would get between them to try to stop them. I knew what Horace could do and didn't want my family hurt. More than once he showed me his gun and threatened to kill everyone in my family. I had a feeling Horace wouldn't hold anything back with them.

Tony had a gun too. He took his responsibility for being the protector of his little sister very seriously and more than once put his life on the line to protect me. Horace would pull out his gun; Tony would pull out his own in response and say, "If you take it out, you'd better use it. If you're not gonna use it, then be careful, 'cause you don't know what will be used on you."

Probably what kept all of us alive in my parents' house was my mom. She was a peacemaker. She'd hound Daddy, telling him, "Babe, that's her husband. Even though we know it's not right, please keep the peace because if you don't, then we might not ever see her again. We might not ever see the children again. Please, hold your tongue so that we'll be able to visit them."

He listened and obeyed her suggestions as much as he could. As did my brother. We all wore masks, living in the same household. Masks that made it look like we were a cohesive family who trusted and respected each other. Masks that allowed a sense of peace while covering up seething anger and threats.

Eventually, CPS allowed us to move back into our townhome, where they made weekly visits. Horace would make sure we were ready for them. The kids would get bathed and dressed in nice clothes. He would always be there for the visits.

He was a saint in front of them. The perfect father and daddy to the outside world. But behind closed doors, it was hell.

Like all devils, Horace knew how to manipulate every person at every moment. You'd end up selling your soul to him before you even knew it was up for negotiation. After CPS would leave, while I was still at the height of my panic thinking they'd find a reason to take my kids away, he'd turn to me reassuringly. "They're not gonna take the kids. We'll just run. That's the only way we'll make this work. Run away from CPS and your parents and go where no one can get to us and mess us up. There are too many people involved in our marriage, and God is telling me we have to move on."

I'm not sure if God specifically told Horace we needed to move to New Orleans, but there were a number of reasons to pick New Orleans.

The major one being all of Horace's family lived there. By that time, that included his parents. Ted's uncontrollable drug habit had caught up with him—or, at least, the dealers he owed had. People in El Paso were looking for him. Because Horace had been one of Ted's suppliers, there was some indication that Horace was also on the hook for missing stock, so moving may have been less about God and saving our family than returning to his roots and not wanting to be found by his angry higher-ups.

My mom begged me not to go. She knew what being in an abusive relationship was like. She had knowledge and resources I could use. But I was so brainwashed, and so fearful of losing my kids, that I couldn't take the hand she offered.

My daddy also tried to encourage me to stay home. He never liked New Orleans, said that it gave him a bad feeling because of all the voodoo and witchcraft. And he was spooked by how the graves were all above ground there. Even more compelling to him, though, as with my mom, was that by that time, Horace had shown his true colors to my family. They all knew what he was about and were terrified to see me go so far away from them. Daddy would be over a thousand miles away from us. He couldn't easily jump in between me and Horace once we left town.

They were so scared for me, but I felt like I had to go. I didn't tell them Horace had threatened numerous times to kill them if I left him. I couldn't be responsible for that. I had to go. So they kissed me on my forehead and sent me on my way, saying all they could do then was pray for me.

I was also fearful of moving. Like my family, I knew what Horace was capable of (or at least I thought I did). Regardless, when we received our income tax refund from our jobs at the Village Inn, we packed up everything we could in the Thunderbird and left. Horace and I had both worked at the Village Inn, he as a cook and I as a waitress. Horace didn't want strangers watching the kids, so we'd do opposite shifts, day and night. When we both had to work, he was willing to let my mom or brother watch the boys. So we saved a little money for our move by having family do childcare, but it was the refund that really paid for it.

The Stick and the Carrot

Texas is mostly flat. Where we lived, we were surrounded by cactus-studded desert. Edging that barrenness are the Franklin Mountains, long and jagged, looking like a giant had started to plow up the earth to plant seeds and then thought better of it.

When we needed to get away, Horace and I would go up to the top of the mountain. We'd take the kids and a treat like ice cream or McDonald's, and we'd sit on the mountaintop and look out over the brown El Paso landscape, all the way into New Mexico and across the Mexican border into Juarez. We could see everything clearly from up there.

I loved it when I didn't have to cook, didn't have to clean, didn't have to have sex, and could just sit on the mountain. It was a sublime treat.

Even the worst abusers aren't mad all the time. There are lulls and good times, positive experiences that help the abused get through the bad. For me, it was those trips to the mountains and the long rides to the ponds in New Mexico to feed the fish. We'd also go to Western Playland to ride the roller coasters, and we'd frequent the Wet 'N' Wild waterpark and scream going down slides as tall as office buildings and then float down the lazy river as if we had no cares in the world. We'd stay all day at Wet 'N' Wild, where we'd eat grilled hot dogs or an avocado sandwich for dinner and drink Slurpees.

Me, blowing kisses at age 15.

Those precious times gave me an opportunity to feel like a little kid again. Those brief respites gave me the breathing room to think maybe this life wasn't so bad. After all, we lived in a nice townhouse. I had a brand-new black Thunderbird. It looked like we had a wonderful life, the kind of life I saw on TV sitcoms.

People never got hit on sitcoms, but in my juvenile mind, I still thought success in life equaled *things*. Besides, when I compared myself to my cousin Julie, who had also lived fast, married young, and had a family, I saw a similar life: she used to get hit a lot too. As did most of my female cousins. They made it seem that what I went through with Horace was normal. I was just like them. Except Julie only drove a Pinto.

There's a cost when the dream of freedom is what defines you. Many of us don't need a master to sell our bodies and souls—we sell ourselves. And we don't notice the invisible mental and emotional chains our jailers wrap around us, especially when we're distracted by physical threats or the opinions of others.

Fear is a weapon of abusers. It gives them control. And they know just what parts of us to threaten. Horace would not only threaten me with his hands; he'd threaten me with a gun. Something I couldn't fend off or run from. Something that wouldn't leave bruises CPS could see. Something that could be fatal with one squeeze of his finger.

When we lived with my parents, his influence weakened, but the gun came out more when we'd be alone. When I would try to leave, he'd put the gun barrel to my head so I could feel the cold steel. He'd put it in my vagina. He'd pull the trigger. I heard the too-loud click of the sprung hammer and my heart would leap to my throat before I realized the gun wasn't loaded, and I wasn't dead. He laughed when I flinched. Then he'd issue threats, but not just about me. My life didn't seem so valuable anymore. No, he'd threaten something more important.

"I'm killing the kids," he'd rasp. "I'm killing your parents. I'm killing everything that's attached to you. If I can't have you, no one can."

So when Horace suggested we move, I was so deep under his spell of fear and manipulation I wasn't thinking rationally anymore. I'm not even sure how much of Monique, as they called me back then, the child bride who'd gotten married with so many dreams and hopes, was left.[1] It didn't matter what anybody said, whether

---

[1] As you'll learn later, I didn't start going by my first name, Katrina, until much later in my life.

that be doctors, CPS, or my mother. If Horace told me I needed to do something, I'd do it. Wholeheartedly.

People get stuck on the "why" of all this. I can't untangle the whole thing, but a few reasons stand out in my mind.

One was the fear of the gun.

Another, I still thought I loved him. This was the man who'd taken my virginity and made me a mother. In the good times, he spoiled me. Bought me cars. Took me places. As the Bible says, two had become one. Love means to give everything up for the happiness of your husband. This was what I was expected to do as a good Christian wife.

And after the CPS incident, Horace had also apologized and started treating me better. That kind of balanced out the promise my mom had made at the same time. She told me she'd help me go back to school and watch my kids if I stayed home with her. Horace won in the end. After being on better behavior for a while, he said he wanted to get better. That if I loved him, I would stay with him and leave town.

The gun was the stick, and it was a pretty big one. His professed love and promise to be a better husband was the carrot. Between them both, I was willing to run away from everything I'd known. I would probably have been willing to leave my kids if that was what Horace said I needed to do. If he'd said we had to kill each other to find peace, I would have done that too. Somehow, following his orders felt safer than resisting. I thought it couldn't get any worse. But whatever it took to protect my kids and my family, I would do.

Church was one place where Horace couldn't completely hide me from the eyes of other people. We still got in the prayer line every Sunday morning, every Friday night, every Tuesday, to get anointed with oil, hoping the Lord would give us favor.

The bruises and CPS couldn't always be hidden from the eyes of the congregation.

Most of the church members thought pretty simply about those problems. They assured me if I prayed, God would answer. That they could help pray the badness out of Horace. One of his favorite excuses was, "The Devil made me do it," and I bought into the idea his devil was something external that could be gotten out of him, exorcized. I thought it was sexy when Horace went down to the altar to pray the Devil out. I thought he wanted to change, that my man was possessed, and when he rolled around on the floor after prayer, I believed the Holy Spirit really did touch him and that tomorrow would be different. It never occurred to me he could be faking it, like I had faked speaking in tongues. It was his religion, the one he'd grown up in, and he always seemed to give it all his respect.

I just couldn't accept that the evil was all him. That no amount of prayer, not even a whole congregation's worth, can pray the devil out of a person who doesn't want him to leave.

My pastor wasn't as optimistic. Our pastor was the superintendent of the church. Always in a suit and tie, always smiling, he was short, chubby, and bald, and he sported glasses. But before we moved to Louisiana, he said something striking that, with all the fuzziness of my memory, I can still recall as clear as day.

"Please don't go," he said. "If you go, God's going to put you through the wilderness."

I'd never heard this before. Confused, I asked, "What's the wilderness?"

He paused and then said solemnly, "God will do whatever He has to do to protect the ones He loves."

I didn't know what he meant. But when I later found myself in the wilderness, I saw it for what it was.

Pain.

Part 2
The Wilderness

Chapter 4
Hard Times in the Big Easy

It took us eight and a half hours to get from El Paso to New Orleans. We looked like a happy family on a great adventure. Horace and I listened to gospel music most of the way—Mississippi Mass Choir, Fred Hammond, and the likes. The boys were in the back, playing and giggling. Every now and then, we'd put on some music for them—a little Barney or Sesame Street. It was so sweet seeing smiles on their little faces every time I looked back at them. They really seemed to enjoy that long car ride! We made a few stops at McDonald's and KFC, and about midway through, we stopped at a rest area so they could stretch and get some fresh air. The trip was so smooth. I could almost believe everything would be different. That we'd really turn into the happy family we resembled on that ride.

I thought maybe that really was possible. After all, the scenery changed more and more the further away from El Paso we drove. We went from the craggy brown mountains and desert scrub of El Paso to the green of New Orleans. So green! That was what struck me the most. So much greenery. And water. You'd drive over the little streams and rivulets of the bayous to get into the city. Vast stretches of mosquito- and gator-filled swamps full of waving reeds and grasses and stunted trees that made the ground look solid, but you knew in the back of your mind if you stepped on that ground, you'd fall right through to unknown depths of murky water.

We moved into a second-floor unit of the Maple Leaf Apartments on the West Bank of New Orleans, near Metairie, across the Lake Pontchartrain Causeway. Horace's cousin, Luke, had helped him pick the place out. I was seventeen and about six months pregnant with my daughter, my third child in as many years. Junior was not quite two and Kenneth not quite one.

It didn't take long for me to agree with my daddy's opinion of New Orleans. Although I can appreciate the city now and actually enjoy going there, when we first arrived, it was a bit creepy to me. Seemed like there was all this talk of voodoo and spells. Then all those cemeteries with the graves above ground!

Eventually, we settled down, and all that didn't bother me much. Horace got a job at a convenience store. I was relieved about that because I didn't want him dealing dope in New Orleans. I wanted a new start, and drugs had gotten us into trouble. I waitressed at a buffet restaurant called Shoney's. Because Horace didn't believe in expensive daycare—or, more accurately, he didn't want anyone intruding on his domain—once more, he worked the graveyard shift, and I worked days, so we traded on childcare. While we hit some hard times affording our bills at first, Horace always managed to provide for his family financially. But his effort to stay on the clean, harder road just couldn't hold up to the easy money of the Big Easy.

I got introduced to the projects for the first time in New Orleans. I'd never been to a project neighborhood in my life, but Horace had a lot of extended family still living in Fisher and St. Thomas projects. The Thomas projects were old, squatting in the middle of New Orleans. And rough. The cops wouldn't go there at night. I'd lived with violence hidden away in the home until this point, but now I understood the everyday violence Horace had grown up around. Drugs were sold openly on the street corners. Fights would break out in front of you. Every so often, a gunshot echoed down the alleys. Even in the daylight, the police would take forever to come out. But I felt safe with Horace. He had his gun, and people stayed away from him. I didn't quite understand, or was in denial about, what that avoidance meant.

Horace's family welcomed me with open arms, but they couldn't get past my age. "Wow!" they'd say, "How did you get married so young?" I got tired of telling the story. We were in love. My mom signed the paperwork. We got married. But I still heard the words "statutory rape" whispered at the edges of conversations. It made me uncomfortable, but I got some reassurance from my new church and Pastor Samuel. He lived a simple life, had no TV, and held church services out of his small house. He told me women got married really young in the days of the Bible, too, and that it was normal for men to have multiple wives and to hit their wives in the Old Testament.

Once we got settled in, like in El Paso, materially, on the surface, our life looked beautiful. A nice three-bedroom apartment, new furniture, nice car. We'd go out to dinner at Shoney's or go get some fish. His family would have crawfish boils and fish fries in the park, with good music, dancing, and games of spades and dominos. The kids would run around, free as birds. It was like a Tyler Perry movie where the grandma would come out and pray, the old auntie would hassle everyone to make the food right, and the men would joke and play dominoes. A family reunion from morning till evening. It was all new and wonderful. I used to look forward to those moments, when I could play kickball with the kids, go down the slide, and swing in the twilight, back and forth, like I was being rocked to sleep.

I felt, during this new honeymoon period of buying new things and getting the place how we wanted it, this was the place where we'd find our own happily ever after. I felt I'd arrived, that I was now in my own household, and it was better than most of my cousins had ever had. Our place was decked out in black and white. We had a big TV entertainment system with surround sound. All the bedrooms were completely furnished—the kids' bedroom was even done up in a Ninja Turtles theme! I got to pick it all out! Horace took me shopping to get it all. It was such a welcome experience. I was living large, even if I had to get used to the Creole food. Coming from El Paso and my mother's house, I was used to Mexican food and spices. Now there I was eating red beans and rice loaded with Creole spices, which was totally different from my mom's, and gumbo, and crawfish.

But all of it was another type of prison. A bubble you lived behind where you could see the world but not interact with it. Lean too hard against that thin glimmery skin, and *pop!* The bubble would burst, and all the ugliness it contained would come spilling out.

I tried not to touch that bubble skin. I didn't want to make Horace too angry. I didn't know what he would do to my kids or even my brother, who, in the oppressive heat of the old city, gave me a form of protection.

Protection

My big brother, Tony, at my mother's urging, followed us to Louisiana despite being recently married. My mother feared Horace would kill me and said I needed Tony's protection. So he quit his job, moved his wife with him to New Orleans, and did the best he could to shield me from Horace. They lived with us at first, staying for about six weeks. It didn't take long for our honeymoon to end, though, and Horace to return to his old self. Tony's wife had to witness the fights between Horace and me, something she hadn't expected ever to do. Sometimes she'd even get involved, to have my back. So Tony would come home from his job and have to defend two women!

Horace wound up kicking them out for coming between us. But my brother took his job protecting me seriously. He moved only five minutes away so he could keep tabs on me and come quickly if I called. He was my way out if it ever came to that.

That move started a trend, a calling for Tony that he couldn't put down. He lives only five minutes from me to this day. My guardian angel. Back then, when things would get tough between Horace and me, I'd call my brother, and he'd come over to our apartment. Often, he'd threaten to take me away, which worked to some extent—or maybe the threat of his own gun worked. Because Horace would plead to me, "I'm sorry. Please don't leave me. You can't take my kids. I'm gonna kill myself if you leave."

Strangely, Horace's mother started getting on him about his abuse. I don't know why she never got involved when we were living in her house in New Mexico. In New Orleans, she and Ted lived across the river from us, and we'd visit them often with the kids. Every time she got on Horace's case for hitting me, he would actually listen to her for a little while. There were a few times when we'd argue that when I got scared, I'd grab the phone and call her, and he'd back down. She may have been a hard taskmaster when I lived in her home, but beating her daughter-in-law, who was now a mother, was a bridge too far. And she was the only person Horace wouldn't cross.

Those two—Tony and Lorraine—were my only protections at first. Then it was only Lorraine because Tony wound up moving back to El Paso. He and his wife decided to divorce—she'd had an affair on him while in New Orleans. Because he moved her out there, he felt he had to move her back to El Paso. That's how my mom raised us. He came to me before he left to let me know he was leaving due to his marriage falling apart but that if I needed anything, he'd just be a phone call away. He kissed me on the head and gave me a big hug goodbye. It was hard for me to let go. I just cried and cried and clung to him. We'd never been apart for very long before. I didn't want to lose him.

So there I was feeling alone in New Orleans. I didn't have any other friends or family. I couldn't make new friends because I couldn't go anywhere but work and church. At work, everyone thought my makeup-free face, permanent ponytail, and knee-length dresses were weird. I didn't even listen to secular music. I also didn't understand just how much my subservience kept people away. I was shy. Wouldn't speak unless spoken to, and when I did speak, I'd never make eye contact, always talking with my head to the ground. I was paranoid that Horace would somehow know if I looked at another man, which would earn me a slap or a humiliating accusation.

At church, as head of our household, Horace ruled my interactions. If I obeyed my husband, I'd be pleasing in the eyes of God. That meant contact with others was limited to prayer.

We had neighbors who tried to help me when we first moved there. They were Hispanic, and it felt like a piece of home when I was near them since the majority of our community was African American. At one point, they even came over and tried to break up one of our fights. That only increased Horace's rage, and he ended up fighting with the neighbor. That was when Horace forbade me to talk to them anymore. Obviously, that friendship was very short.

I'd only talk to my parents in the middle of the night, when Horace was at work, to avoid backlash. I wouldn't tell them the bad stuff because I didn't want them coming out to see us, since I didn't know what the repercussions would be. I wanted to protect them, so I pretended everything was better. Some nights, after I hung up the phone, I'd go into my kids' room and just hold them. Some nights, I'd cry myself to sleep.

We lived in a comfortable uncomfortable pattern of violence and reconciliation. He'd beat or threaten me and then buy me gifts the next day and tell me he loved me, that I was beautiful.

He'd say, "I'm so sorry. I'll never do it again."

He'd say, "If you leave me, I'm gonna kill your whole family. We'll all go to heaven."

Or he'd say, "If you go, I'm going to kill myself," and he'd put his gun, a 9 mm Beretta Black, to his head. Those nights, he'd sleep with that gun on his nightstand.

It was a roller coaster I couldn't get off. My husband had trapped me. Chained me emotionally and mentally, even if I wasn't imprisoned by actual cold steel bars.

But here's a crazy thing: if you ride roller coasters long enough, one day, you realize you've stopped screaming. You learn to get used to the wild and scary ride. I figured out how to manage his abuse and his threats, all the ups and downs. There was only so much Horace could do to someone who did mostly what he wanted.

Unfortunately, while I learned how to take a punch and marshal my protections, there existed within reach others with no such resources: my kids.

The Innocents

When we moved, Junior was just over one and a half, and Kenneth was about nine months. At those sweet young ages, Horace was of the opinion they should "know better" and do exactly as they were told. He never gave them slack, was always heavy-handed. Strict.

The first time Horace snapped big after we moved to New Orleans was because the kids were playing too loudly. They weren't being wild or anything. They always played like you'd expect little ones to play: they'd run in circles in the apartment and laugh or sit and play with cars, Legos, or their Ninja Turtles. Maybe once in a while, they'd kick a ball, but not often. Horace didn't like us to go outside. Actually, he didn't *let* us go outside unless he went with us. One day he was asleep on the couch after working the night shift. He always slept there so we couldn't sneak out without him hearing us. I tried to keep the kids on the quiet side, but they woke him up by accident. Their toddler screaming must have rubbed him the wrong way because he got really rough with them. He took off his belt, wrapped it around his fist, and punched them in the chest. On the first hit, they each were so stunned they needed to catch their breath before they cried.

"Shut up!" Horace yelled. "Just shut the hell up!"

"They're just babies!" I tried to defend them. "You're going to break all their ribs! Of course they're crying. That hurts!"

He rounded on me. "Now you shut up, Monique, or I'll deal the same to you!"

"Hit me." I gathered both whimpering boys in my arms, wanting to shield them with my body and love. "They're innocent. Hit me, but don't hit them."

"Stop sticking up for them! I'm not raising sissies. They're men. You can't baby them."

Yes, he called my toddler boys "men." That wasn't the first time he'd punched them like that, dead in the middle of the chest, justifying that they were young men and should be able to take the blows. He ignored my pleas to stop, so I'd use my body as their shield.

I guess to Horace, violence was just part of being a human. But I couldn't stand it. I'd intercede as much as I could. Sometimes, I also got hit as he tried to get through the cage I tried to make of my arms and legs, tucking my pregnant belly between me and the boys. And I waited for the inevitable moment I'd go numb to the pain.

Horace blamed the worst of these incidents on his diabetes. He said he had blackouts where he'd commit the worst of the violence. I was only seventeen and didn't understand how the disease worked. This was my first encounter with it. I only knew it was life-threatening (because that was what he told me). And that it led to comas. When we lived with my family, they found him a couple of times in diabetic comas. They could have just let him die but instead would call the ambulance. I didn't understand then that he didn't have to go into those comas, that they were a result of him not managing his disease. I just thought it was a symptom of how bad the illness was and how much he needed me. And I thought they explained his blackout rages.

Later, I'd learn bipolar disorder ran in Horace's family. That might have been part of his problem, too, though most people who struggle with that condition don't hurt other people. So I really don't know why he was so violent. Violence was just part of him, and he easily let me witness that side of him, so he must have felt that level of behavior—the level I witnessed—was OK for him to indulge in. He must have thought it acceptable.

But there was another level, a deeper one, that even he knew was too far because he hid it. As with Kenneth's burned feet, the bruises from those sessions of violence were subtle, hidden. Kenneth, of course, with the question of where he got his lighter skin tone hanging over his head, would bear the brunt of it. He always had little marks and bruises. I'd ask where they came from, and Horace would tell me with a solemn face that Junior did it.

As I look back now, after having shaken the fog of my own captivity, I realize I was in denial. I didn't want to believe Horace was the one causing those marks and bruises on my baby. I didn't want to see it. Because then, I might have forced myself to do something or become a person I couldn't live with. To save my soul, I couldn't believe it.

Then came Shaniqua.

Shaniqua

I received the majority of my prenatal care in El Paso at the state hospital at Thomason before we moved. I was just about to turn seventeen when we moved, and the whole process and unfamiliarity of New Orleans delayed finding another ob-gyn. It wouldn't be until the tail end of my pregnancy, at eight or nine months, that I resumed care, which was pretty much when I had my third child, a daughter, at the hospital in New Orleans Parish.

She was my first girl. She was small but healthy and perfectly normal, with a full head of black hair. We took her home in a little pink dress with a matching pink headband with a big bow on it. We named her Shaniqua because that name had significance to the Muslims. Even though we were steeped in the Pentecostal church, Horace was fascinated by Islam, something his mother would have nothing to do with. In fact, he wound up learning not to talk about his interest in it with his mom. Many of the people he hung out with in New Orleans were Muslim, though. He'd started studying the Quran and practiced some of its teachings, like not eating pork, and eventually he wanted to convert. He liked that American Islam was rooted in the Black community. Horace didn't like white people. He borrowed the Muslim epithet "white devils" and used it whenever he talked about the trouble white people would give Black men.

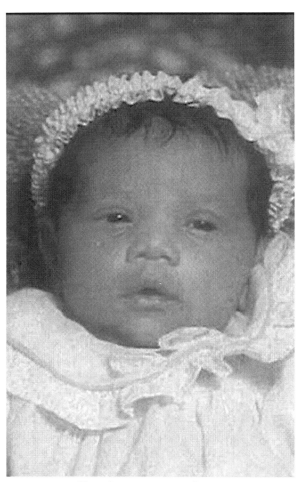

Shaniqua as a newborn

Shaniqua was our little princess. We'd dress her like a doll, and Horace would get after the boys for even looking at her wrong, though they, too, were happy to have a baby sister. Right after she was born, Horace seemed to mellow. He acted like an excellent dad. He'd come home from his graveyard shift, play with the kids, and then just hold Shaniqua in his arms. I truly thought things had turned a corner with the presence of this sweet little girl. She was like an angel who brought peace to our little family. That peace didn't extend to El Paso, though. My parents didn't come to see the new baby right away. They were still unhappy that I was in New Orleans.

Everything changed when Shaniqua was three months old.

As usual, I came directly home after work. Usually, if I worked an early shift, I'd be home no later than three or four in the afternoon, though sometimes I'd stay later to get overtime or to reach my tip amount goal. Horace would always collect all my earnings and tips to help cover rent and bills and whatever else we needed. He knew how much I should make on a typical day. I never kept a dime of my own money. I didn't even have credit cards in my name. Granted, I wasn't a legal adult who could have credit cards yet, but even if I had been, as head of the household, he would have had full control.

That day, I was exhausted. I'd worked a double shift. I wanted to get out of my uniform—restaurant polo shirt, black pants, apron, rubber nonskid shoes—that always smelled of stale restaurant food no matter how much I washed it. I dragged myself into the shower, threw on my pajamas, and snuggled in my bed with my kids, enjoying my time with them while Horace went through his final work prep routine and left. It was a normal handoff, and he didn't mention anything about a rough day at home.

I put the boys to bed only a little while later and returned to my and Horace's room, where Shaniqua, at three months old, was still asleep in a bassinet in the middle of our king-sized bed. The sheets and comforter were jet black, as if reflecting the mood of the outside world that I watched on TV.

Although it was July, the news was still focused on the April 15 Oklahoma City bombing that had happened earlier that year. No one could understand how a terrorist attack could happen on US soil. It was something unthinkable. Unbelievable. The Alfred P. Murrah Federal Building had been reduced to a cloud of debris. I thought the Lord was on his way down, fulfilling the warning I'd always hear from the church: "We're living in the End Times."

Spastic movement jolted my attention to Shaniqua. All I could think, as my vision narrowed to the little body next to me, bathed in the light coming from the TV, was, *Why is she twitching*?

I called Horace at work. "Did you notice Shaniqua is twitching? She's shaking every five minutes."

"No," Horace said shortly. "She was fine."

I hung up, but something didn't feel right. This was not a cute baby dream twitch. This was scary shaking, at regular intervals. Like a seizure.

I was anxious, nervous, and on edge, like every parent who sees a potential hospital visit in the middle of the night with three young children in tow. You don't want an illness to be bad enough to make that call, but you can't dismiss the evidence of your own eyes. I called my mom and asked for her advice.

"Monica," she said firmly, "this isn't right. Babies don't twitch like that. You have to take her to the hospital."

I had my driver's license, but tonight, because of my double shift, I hadn't dropped Horace off and returned home. Instead, he'd taken the Thunderbird, our only car. So a neighbor let all of us pile into his car and drove us to the local ER.

I explained to the hospital staff that I'd come home from work and found her twitching, and it wouldn't stop. The doctors took her back to a room, and I was asked to wait with the kids in the waiting room. Those little colored wire racks with the chunky block beads populated the area like cheerful twisted bird cages, and they worked to keep the boys occupied.

Finally, they let me into the back with the kids and started questioning me. Did she fall? Did something happen? Did she roll off the bed?

The questions wouldn't stop, and I was scared. I kept repeating, "I don't know! I was at work!"

I called Horace to see what might have happened, but he said he didn't recall anything that stood out. "Listen," he said, "I'll get there as soon as somebody gets here to relieve me. Whatever you do, don't say anything else to anyone. Just stop talking."

The hospital staff kept at me, though. The doctors knew the answers they were looking for already. They knew what they were looking at and were confident with their diagnosis.

They ramped up the questions.

"Did someone hit her? Was she shaken?" Shaken baby syndrome was frequently spoken about in the news. I knew what they were talking about, but I didn't understand how that was possible. The questions continued—the *accusing* questions continued. "Did somebody drop her? She doesn't have any bruises on the outside. Was she shaken? Who did this? How did this happen?"

I kept saying, "I don't know!" because I didn't know. And I just wanted to know what was wrong with her. Was she going to be OK? Was she going to live? Why weren't they telling me what was happening to her instead of asking me all these questions that I didn't have answers for? Asking questions with accusation in their tones as well as the looks on their faces.

Soon I found out why they were so concerned.

A massive bump on Shaniqua's head was unusual for the normal tumbles babies might have, they said. A fall, even a bad one from being accidentally dropped, couldn't explain it. Then they told me she had multiple injuries. She was in such bad shape they were transferring her to the Children's Hospital in New Orleans. They didn't share specifics because they were already getting the authorities involved.

At some point, Horace, expressing concern and confusion, had joined us, so he drove me and the boys to the Children's Hospital. Shaniqua was airlifted, taken away by a helicopter. It was a quiet car ride, except for the requests for prayers. We called everyone we knew so they could help pray for us.

Instead of a medical team, eight cops met us at the hospital. They immediately separated us, me one way and Horace and the boys another. They had us take turns waiting with the boys. Scared and confused, I cried until my whole body shook with sobs. "I just want to be with my daughter!" I kept yelling, but it took a long time for anyone to take me to see her.

When they finally allowed me up to her room, it was hard to actually see her. There were tubes all over her, a ventilator beeping in the background along with other machines whirring and making noises and flashing digital numbers. All that technology was trying to keep the tiny limp body in the middle of the big hospital bed alive. That was when they gave me the rundown of her injuries: a broken vein in her eye, six broken ribs, two broken legs, and a skull fracture. All were internal, so I hadn't been able to see them, just their consequences.

They told me if I'd gotten to the ER any later, she would have been dead already.

How *did* this happen?

The hospital staff asked me if we had any money for a hotel. When I told them no, they said we could stay as a whole family at the Ronald McDonald House on the hospital campus for free because we couldn't stay in the hospital with the two boys. By now I knew we, the parents, were under investigation for child abuse.

How did *this* happen? I knew *how* to answer that question. I just didn't *want* to answer it.

The first thing I did when the boys and I settled in our room at the Ronald McDonald House was call my mom, daddy, and brother. I needed them more than ever.

Horace was stoic, calm. Dead calm. He kept saying everyone didn't know what they were talking about. He told me to pray.

For everything I'd been through, everything I'd witnessed, I'd convinced myself it would never come to this. I'd convinced myself that I was doing what was best for my children in the eyes of God by keeping our family together with their father, who could provide for them.

The next morning, I remember I put on an ivory dress with flowers all over it. Something hopeful, for my daughter. I went to the hospital when visiting hours started to see Shaniqua. But the staff told me, "We're sorry, but we can't allow you to see your daughter anymore."

However, there was a little angel back there, a nurse who knew how distressed I was, that all I wanted to do was look at my baby girl one more time. She approached me and said, "I'm going to take you back, even though I'm not supposed to. You can be there for just five minutes, and then I'm going to have to get you out or I'll get in trouble."

She took me back to a room filled with all these machines. There in the middle was my baby girl. So still and small, tubes snaking all over her body. I didn't know if she would live or die. I held her tiny hand, cried, and prayed, I kissed her forehead and begged God to protect her. Soon, too soon, that nurse came back and said I had to go. As broken-hearted as I was in that moment, I remember being so appreciative of that one act of grace by that nurse.

I walked out of the room, hearing the steady beeping of the machines. They sounded like wounded animals lost somewhere in the undergrowth.

Pastor Moore was right. I'd entered the wilderness.

Retribution

Shaniqua, thank God who watched over her, lived through her ordeal.

Her parents, the people charged with protecting her, had a different reckoning.

The hospital advised us to go home and get cleaned up before we went to the police station. I took a shower and fed the kids, but I wasn't hungry. When we went to the station, Horace, still calm, told me not to talk to anyone without an attorney present. I didn't understand. I hadn't done anything wrong. Had I? Actually, I had. I had come to Louisiana and brought my kids with me. That kept playing in my head. I should have stayed home.

CPS met us at the station and shepherded Junior and Kenneth away. Then we were questioned separately.

After doctors had determined this was an abuse case, they called in a detective, a white lady named Katie. Detective Katie questioned me alone for six to eight hours straight. After she ran me ragged, she asked calmly, "Do you know who you married?"

"I don't understand what you're saying!" I was so scared and confused and just plain exhausted. Nothing made sense.

"Well, your husband has a rap sheet a mile long." That surprised me. I knew of the drug dealing (though I had trusted him that he'd quit), but the robbery and other crimes they showed me were new to me. "He manipulated you," she persisted. "But you did one thing wrong: you stayed. You stayed after your first CPS case in El Paso. Why didn't you leave then?"

Her question echoed the one I'd been asking myself. Why didn't I leave him then? I told her I was scared. I told her the Bible said I was supposed to follow my husband.

But at that moment, with Shaniqua's life in the balance, I didn't really know why I'd stayed with a monster. I blamed myself for putting my kids in harm's way. "I should have stayed with my parents," I whispered.

And now it was too late, and I would be judged.

They brought the boys back to me. They played by my feet—Junior with his big, cute smile, and Kenneth all chubby and with curly hair, looked so sweet, so innocent. Every time they'd see me cry during Katie's questioning, they'd hug me and wipe the tears from my face.

But then Detective Katie dealt a bigger blow, one I couldn't fend off. "Do you have anybody here who could take the kids?"

"No. Why do my kids have to be taken from me?"

She looked me straight in the eyes. "I don't want to do this to you, but I'm going to have to arrest you as an accessory after the fact."

At that time, child abuse cases were through the roof in New Orleans. Kids were dying, and the authorities were not in the mood to be kind. What I ended up being accused and convicted of was accessory to attempted murder, a big crime with a harsh sentence. "Because you're the mother," they said, "and all this could have been prevented if you'd left the first time the abuse occurred."

The first time.

I should have left after Kenneth's burned feet.

No. I should have left after I ended up in the hospital the first time.

No, after the first time I was hit.

I should have.

But I didn't.

And now would come my punishment.

They arrested both Horace and me at the station. I could hear my boys screaming, "Mommy? Mommy! *Mommy! Please don't leave me!*" They each clamped onto my legs as I had to walk away from them. I promised them everything would be all right, but I had no idea if that was a hollow promise. It was one of the hardest days of my life.

In desperation, I called my parents. "You gotta come! You gotta come get them!"

They were the only people I had. Horace called his parents, but they didn't want to get involved. I think they saw the whole thing as an embarrassment to the family. And I didn't want them to take the kids anyway, knowing Ted's drug habit. I thought foster care would be better. I begged the police to give the kids to my parents.

Up until the last moment, when they separated us at the police station, Horace had insisted we'd be OK. "We'll get through this," he promised me. "Just don't talk to anyone." His words would prove ironic since they wouldn't let us communicate with each other after that. No visits. No calls. Not even letters.

Ironic, also, that the one thing I thought proved my goodness to God, staying together, was the thing that separated us in the end.

There's an old belief that all hell breaks loose once Catholic school girls go off to college. The chains of family expectations and strict school rules are shed with the plaid uniforms, and the sheltered teenagers can't handle it. It's like they've lived all their young lives in a soda bottle that's been shaken, and now the top's come off. The bad choices come from not having practice at making bad choices when they're young—they've never been allowed to make their own rules or decisions, so they don't know how to make good ones. And now they are near-adults, with near-adult temptations and consequences.

Take the chains of propriety off, and you get hellions, or so the old folks say. Similar things were said of slaves, as a justification by Southern slaveholders for keeping them in bondage. Set them free, and it would just be chaos.

Freedom and chains. Two ends of a spectrum of control, where one person always has total power over another. I think we need freedom in our lives, at each stage of our lives. The freedom to make mistakes with limited consequences—or at least informed consequences.

Actually, to gain the knowledge to know when to stay and when to leave.

Booked

I got booked with a red wristband, to mark the severity of my crime. Yellow was for misdemeanors. Orange for felonies. Red was for murder.

Not knowing exactly where my children were going in the hands of CPS and isolated from Horace, I began my journey to prison when the police put me in a holding cell with other women in the back of the station. I was still in the girlish flowered sundress I wore when I got up that morning to go to the hospital to check on Shaniqua. My hair was pulled back in a ponytail. I looked like a cheerful bouquet you'd give to your granny, except my eyes were bloodshot red and puffy from all the crying.

I kept quiet in that cell, just waited for whatever would come next. I wouldn't eat. I just cried. Cried and cried. Unable to stop.

I felt my youth acutely under the hardened eyes of my cellmates. "Little Red," they'd breathe from the corners of the stark cell covered in chipped paint. "Little Reeeeeddd...what'd you do to get back here? Where did you go astray?"

I didn't answer. I was nervous. I was scared. I'd been free that morning with three young kids, a husband, and a black Thunderbird. Now, at seventeen, I was an accessory to murder and a prisoner. Where did my life go wrong?

Being honest with myself, I had to admit, at least in my own head, that I had been living a dream life, a fantasy. I had let myself believe that in spite of being beaten up, abused, and misused, I was living a dream life in my fully furnished apartment. I asked God why I didn't listen to my parents. Why didn't I just listen? My daughter was about to die because I didn't listen. My kids weren't with me anymore because I didn't listen. I had learned that lesson now. What was next? What was God trying to show me?

Chapter 5
Defined by a Number

Not quite forty-eight hours after I first took my daughter to the hospital—less than twenty-four hours after being arrested—my bail was set at $50,000. I wasn't able to pay it. I didn't have any money in my name, nor did I have anyone willing to pay it. I had no option but to go to prison. This time, the prison wasn't built just from mental and emotional chains. It had steel bars and razor wire.

With the whispers of the other women in the holding cell still slinking around my skull and the red band feeling like it was burning a permanent scar on my wrist, I was taken back to a big old pod with sixty bunk beds. There was one row of thirty on one side of the room and another row of thirty on the other side. At one end of the pod was a TV; at the other were the showers and commodes. They were wide open, with no doors or curtains. Everything I saw was stainless steel: the commodes, the shower fixtures, the beds. Everything was open. Everything exposed.

The guards watched us take our clothes off. Then they told us to bend over, spread our butt cheeks, and cough three times. I guess it was a way to make sure we were clean and not hiding drugs or something. After that they gave us open-toed sandals and orange jumpsuits to put on. On the back of the jumpsuit was printed in big black letters OPP, which stood for Orleans Parish Prison.

I was given a top bunk. I climbed up and just cried all night long.

The Pod

Since my time in Orleans Parish Prison, there have been updates and changes to the building structures.[2] So I guess things are a little different now. When I was there, the pods were supposed to be for inmates who'd committed lighter crimes or who, for whatever reason, would only be there for a short amount of time. I was in it for about forty-five days (the first time) before being transferred over to Templeman III, which was where the people charged with heavy cases, the criminal felonies, would go.

We had no first names in the pod. As the cold fluorescent lights signaled day, there was a roll call, the first of three every day. I'd hear "Kennedy!" and answer, which was about all I said at first. The rest of my time during those first couple of weeks, I cried, read my Bible, prayed, and kept to myself—that is, when I wasn't running up my parents' phone bill by calling them collect every fifteen minutes.

The mothers, as I learned they were called, were older inmates who'd sit at the ends of their beds and talk all day. They'd bring meals to me, but I wouldn't eat. Finally, one day, this older lady came to my bunk and said, "Little Red, you're going to have to eat." She sat down near me. "Here, let me do your hair."

Maybe because she had some kind of maternal energy, I trusted her. I let her put braids in my hair. She worked on my hair, plaiting it, and promised me I'd be all right. Another woman, a younger one,

---

[2] Perhaps most notably were the changes after Hurricane Katrina came through in 2005. While the prison was never known for its outstanding treatment of its inmates, no one would ever have expected what the staff did to the prisoners during that category 5 storm. They abandoned them. They left 640 human beings to figure out how to survive with no access to food, fresh water, or even ventilation. There is no official death count, but Human Rights Watch claims 517 prisoners are "unaccounted for." https://www.hrw.org/news/2005/09/21/new-orleans-prisoners-abandoned-floodwaters

let me borrow pens and paper so I could write letters back home. She explained the commissary to me.

The commissary was a store of sorts. If you had family or friends on the outside, they could put money on "your book." Then you'd get to go to the commissary and use that money to buy things. It took two weeks before I could get my name on the commissary books. The system isn't in a hurry to do that because most people who land in the pod are there just overnight and get out on bail, so they don't need it. In the interim, I was stuck borrowing paper from that kind woman and using a very generic kind of soap and shampoo when I showered.

We could only shower in the mornings, and it had to be fast because they'd run out of hot water. No one had to tell me to be fast, though. I hated showering. There was no privacy. There were about eight shower heads lined up on the wall with no curtains or walls—you were completely open and exposed whenever you wanted to shower. Everybody had to shower in the morning—all sixty of us! Some of the other women would whistle at me. Others would catcall, "Little Red! You're so pretty!" I'd cover up as much as I could as I washed. I was so scared. So intimidated. All I could think of, especially at first, was what I'd learned about from movies—what If I got raped? I quickly learned to be one of the first to get in, very early in the morning, when there were fewer people awake. Opposite the showers was a row of toilets. So you could be using a toilet with someone showering right in front of you—both of you could watch each other. It was crazy!

It took me a few weeks to acclimate. I seldom left my bunk at the beginning unless it was for a hated shower or to call my parents. I called them—collect—as much as I could. They'd give me updates on the kids. Very limited updates because Shaniqua was still in the hospital and my boys in foster care. My mom would assure me she and my daddy were doing everything they could to secure custody of my children. She promised me we had nothing to worry about. That Shaniqua would make it and be fine. That she'd get my boys,

That we'd all be back together soon. Eventually, we'd run out of things to say on the call, but I wouldn't want it to end. Hearing her voice was the closest thing to home I had in that environment—an environment filled with monsters, as I originally saw it.

You had to hold onto whatever you had. They gave each one of us a towel, a blanket, a pillow, that generic soap and shampoo, a brush, and one roll of toilet paper that you had to carry with you each time you needed to go to the bathroom. As meager as it all was, people would steal things, especially blankets in the winter when it got cold and towels any time of year. And once your towel was gone, that was it. You didn't get another one unless someone you knew left and gave it to you.

At one point, I was able to move from a top bunk to a bottom one and then used my towel like a curtain to give me some sense of privacy. And eventually, I had access to the commissary. Things shifted, and I realized I was scared less frequently. I was getting used to being in prison.

My family and Daniel, my first love, put money on my books so I could buy "luxuries" like Dial soap, Oreos, and pens and paper. More treasures to hoard and keep safe from others. But I also paid back everyone who had been nice to me. Like the older African American lady who'd plaited my hair. She was heavyset and would give me candy or Ramen noodles she got from the commissary before I had money on my books. She'd been in for a couple of years, waiting to see what her fate would be. Waiting for her day in court. When I started talking to others, I realized she wasn't the only one. So many people had no idea how much longer they'd be there. They were like me. I started speaking to more people then, making connections, trying to make it feel more like home, I guess.

On a daily basis, people's names would be called. Sometimes it seemed like every fifteen minutes a last name was called on the intercom with "rolling out." That meant they were being set free. Every time I heard a noise from the intercom, I'd pray, *Please say "Kennedy, rolling out!"* I never heard those words. Though I did get "out" occasionally—to go to court, which was where I often saw Horace.

Seeing Horace

"How you doing, Monique?" Horace would ask whenever we had to go to court. He would be brought into the holding cell area and placed on the men's side of a dividing wall. I would be taken to the same cell and placed on the women's side, and I would press up against the cement wall opposite him. We were close enough there that we could hear each other talk. I struggled through those conversations, trying to make sense of what I was thinking, feeling, and doing. I hated him for what he'd done to our daughter, for breaking apart our family, for putting me in prison...yet part of me felt a sense of relief each time I heard his voice—that familiar voice asking me how I was doing. Each time I had a chance to press against the wall and know he was on the other side, I felt a strange sense of comfort.

We'd get about fifteen or twenty minutes to talk that way. It was the only time we ever communicated, as we were not allowed to write letters or call each other. Technically, we weren't allowed to talk to each other then, but often when the guards would do a check, they really didn't care.

He'd ask me how I was doing and then check in on the kids. My parents refused to contact him, so I would relay the information they'd tell me. Before we parted, he'd tell me to get a public defender or hire a lawyer, which was funny because he knew I had no money. Then he'd add a promise, which, as time wore on, felt like a threat: "Don't say anything. They don't have any evidence. We're going to beat this case and be together again."

We'd have to appear before the court together. They'd call us up: "Kennedy versus Kennedy," meaning Shaniqua Kennedy versus her parents.

The session would last only about five minutes because one of the first questions asked by the judge was, always, "What's going on

81

with the baby?" For the longest time, there was no change, so the court would be rescheduled. They couldn't charge us with anything until they were assured Shaniqua would live or she would die. Our charges depended on her state.

We'd be escorted back to the holding cells, where we'd take up our seats as before, across the wall from each other, and continue talking.

That scenario was repeated several times when I was in the pod. It became the only thing that was *not* part of my daily routine and life there.

Templeman III

"Kennedy!" I heard my name called out one day over the intercom. Could it be my release? No Turned out, I was getting transferred. "Get your stuff. You're being transferred."

"Where am I going?"

"Over to the Templeman side."

Templeman was where the people who'd committed major crimes went. Why were they taking me there? No one would tell me. I just had to do as I was told. I gathered up what few belongings I had. Once more, I was filled with terror about the unknown ahead of me. I'd finally almost become comfortable in the pod. I had a few people I trusted and spoke to. What was going to happen to me now?

The mother who took care of me came over to say goodbye. I gave her about half my commissary purchases to say thank you for being so good to me.

"Where do you think I'm going?" I asked her.

"Baby," she said, "you're going to be OK. You're going to have your own little apartment."

She meant a prison cell. I wouldn't be in an open pod anymore. My freedom would become even more restricted.

Most likely, I was transferred because I still had on a red band, which meant I didn't belong in the pod with the women who'd committed misdemeanors. My case wasn't moving fast enough for the court to officially sentence me anywhere, so they just sent me over. Probably needed to give my bed to someone else.

Whatever the reason, I had to go through the whole process of being stripped of my dignity again. I had to strip, spread my cheeks, and cough three times to prove I wasn't smuggling any drugs. Then, once more in my orange jumpsuit and sandals, they put handcuffs on my wrists and chains around my ankles. Soon enough a guard grabbed my right arm and escorted me out.

Once again, I was filled with fear. By then I knew where I was going: Templeman III. It was where there were actual cells. It was where the "really bad" people went. The women in the pod with me were in for prostitution, minor theft, that kind of thing. Who would I be imprisoned with next?

I was put in unit 4, cell block 2, cell #3. I was escorted up the stairs, arriving on the floor where a couple dozen women just stared at me, watching me as I was taken to my cell. It was like being a kid, afraid of the way the lions looked at you from the other side of the bars at a zoo.

I was placed in my cell and did what I'd done that first day in the pod. I cried and cried and cried. I felt so small, so scared again. After I got that out of my system, I realized I had my cell to myself, and I set to work to make the best of it. I took the bottom bunk, doubled up the sheets to try to make that thin, ratty mattress soft. It was so cold over there. They gave me an extra blanket. But I was still cold.

There were two beds, the bunks, in each of the cells. There was a mirror made of plastic so you couldn't break it and use sharp glass on anyone. And everything else was made of stainless steel: a toilet and a sink. I could see the TV from my cell, so I decided to just stay in my cell, by myself, and get acclimated.

Someone brought food to me that I didn't eat. And another mother type came around and asked why I was there. I replied in Spanish saying I didn't speak English. I had steeled myself to think I would just stay tough, stay to myself, and bide my time. But that night something happened that I soon discovered happened every night.

As soon as the lights went out, that first night I was gripped with fear of what could possibly happen in the darkness. But then an anonymous person burst out singing "He's that Kind of Friend" by Walter Hawkins. I knew that song from church! When she finished, someone started a prayer! I had hope. While I didn't know any of those people, I now had hope because there was something we shared—me and them. There was something familiar that almost felt like a bond. After the prayer, they all yelled goodnight to each other.

I was safe that night. When I woke up the next morning, I felt hopeful. These women sang songs about God. They said prayers before going to sleep! I had money on my books, steady money coming in that I could use in the commissary. I would be able to survive this.

I ventured out to the common area of our cell block unit and asked around about going to the commissary. Someone explained they did it differently there—you didn't go to the commissary; it came to you. You had to fill out this green piece of paper that listed everything available. You'd mark what you wanted and turn it in to the person in charge of it. They had different things available to them in Templeman—things we didn't have access to in the pod. I guess it was because we were expected to be there a long time. I was able to order softer toilet paper and socks. But I needed help placing the order. I asked the woman who'd come to speak to me when I was first brought in.

"Oh, so you wanna talk now?" she laughed.

"I don't know how to do this! Can you help with the commissary?" I asked. And she did. Her name was Brenda, but we called her Mama B. She explained the different soaps—what would make my skin itchy and dry and what was better. She helped me break the ice with the others there.

Still sweetly haunted by that voice singing the night before, I asked who it was.

"Oh, that's Faith!" someone answered me. "You'll love her. Come meet her."

And then I was introduced to Faith. A bright lady in her thirties, a little heavyset. She had three big plaits in her hair and a do-rag holding it back, and she had the prettiest face. She was in for drugs and battery but was so nice to me.

"Thank you for singing that song" I told her. "It was what I needed to hear. Do you know who gave the prayer?"

That was when I found out Mama B was the woman who'd said the prayer. Faith explained they always said their prayers at night, and she always sang—unless she was having an off day and was unhappy. But she said someone else would sing.

Turned out, Mama B was in for attempted murder and assault. She had the sweetest soul. I could only think that something terrible had happened to her for her to wind up doing something that landed her in prison.

Daily Life in Templeman III

On a typical day back there in the cell block, we'd hear a big buzzer around 7:00 a.m.. The cell doors would all open automatically, and the guards would come in for morning roll call right after their shift change. They'd do a roll call after every shift change, three per day. The clang of a metal door would herald their arrival. We'd get out of bed and stand in front, just like you see on TV, and yell out our number—you didn't just lose your freedom in Templeman III; you lost your name. We only had names among each other; according to the prison, we were just numbers.

After that first roll call, we could go back to our beds or get ready for the day until it was time for breakfast an hour later. I'd use that time to pray, wash my face, read my Bible, and write letters or journal.

Breakfast could be grits, or a boiled egg, or cereal and milk. The last we'd sometimes save and eat throughout the day. They also served Kool-Aid, which somehow they made to taste like medicine. It was terrible! As a treat, we'd get bacon. I had barely eaten while in the pod and had lost a lot of weight. I was probably around ninety-five pounds. That morning Mama B took me around and introduced me to everyone, she also sat with me for breakfast. We had grits, sausage, an apple, and milk. I only took a little bit of plain grits.

"Little Red," Mama B said. Somehow my name had traveled with me. "You don't want to eat that like that. Here!" She tried to put a square of cheese on my plate.

"No. I don't eat that."

"You're so skinny! You got to eat before you fly away. We gotta put some meat on that little body." Next thing I knew, I was learning how to eat in prison. I was introduced to cheese in my grits, and at first I didn't understand where it came from. They didn't serve cheese with grits at breakfast.

"Every day something different comes," Mama B said. "When the cheese comes, you keep it."

"How? Where?" It wasn't like I had access to a fridge or anything.

I got my answer—my training—from my cellmate, who arrived on my third day. She taught me how to use the toilet or the sink in my cell as a refrigerator. Because they were made of stainless steel, they stayed cold. We'd save cheese and butter, put it in plastic (they delivered our commissary orders in plastic bags), and then crumble it over our grits to make them taste better. Sometimes, we'd get lucky and they'd give us boiled eggs that we could keep for a full day if we wrapped them up real tight.

Lunch was always a sandwich and some fruit. Dinner would be potatoes or rice and some kind of meat with gravy—lots of gravy. They'd also give you two pieces of bread that I'd use to make sandwiches with the peanut butter and jelly I'd get from the commissary.

After breakfast, you could watch the one TV in the common area by the commissary. The common room was shaped like a U, with two floors open to it so you could see everyone leaving and going to their cells. There were two payphones on one wall and several metal tables shaped like picnic tables. We'd watch movies—something we all agreed to. *The Price Is Right* was on every day. As were *The Young and Restless* and *The Bold and the Beautiful* soap operas. A highlight when I was in was when the BET Awards came on. If you were lucky and had a cell in the middle of the U like I did, you could watch the TV from your bed.

If they weren't watching TV, you'd see people playing dominoes and cards. There was always this one mother with a do-rag over her head who'd slam her cards down. *Bam!* So much noise between the cards clamming and dominoes hitting the metal tables. It was a totally different atmosphere than what I was used to in the pods. I was nervous among them at first, feeling like the outsider that I knew I was. Eventually, though, I loosened up and learned how to play real dominoes and spades, games I'd watched on the outside but never participated in.

If you wanted to take a shower, you'd have to go to the shower rooms upstairs. Finally, there was a little bit of privacy! Not much, but there was a shower curtain that offered a smidge of privacy. I would take my time putting on lotion and doing my facial with Dial soap. I learned that if you rubbed that soap on your face and left it until it dried, it would dry out your pores and prevent pimples. It worked wonders.

I could wrap a towel around me before leaving the shower. It almost felt like a luxury not having to be naked in front of everybody. And in my cell, I could hang my towel over the bars and get some privacy to use the toilet there, too. I have never taken a towel for granted ever since!

After the morning routine, we could go back to the common room and play dominoes or spades or go to our cells for a nap.

We'd get one hour outside each day, where we could walk the yard and get some fresh air or play volleyball. If it was raining, we could go to the gym. Because the Orleans Parish Prison housed both males and females, we had the chance to glimpse the opposite sex every time we went outside. The guys would stand in the window and try to talk to us. Some of them were perverts, but others would yell, "Hey! Write me! Here's my number!" You could do prison mail with them if you had their number. But I didn't want to at that time because I was still married.

There were no services to speak of to break up the monotony, except for optional rotating church services and prayer groups. I went to every church service. They usually happened about twice a week, and they were unique in that the whole population could attend. We'd all come together then. I looked forward to it so much, and those few times we didn't have a service were such a letdown for me. There were no mental health counselors to see, only a psychiatrist who'd handle the medications of the people who were schizophrenic or bipolar.

The timing for our schedule was strict—here's when you wake up; here's when you take a shower; here's when you eat, when you sleep, when you go outside. Everything had a time limit. Calls. TV. Outside. Meals. That was when you understood that part of freedom included choosing how to spend your time. That was when I learned the first time that freedom ain't free—I paid for my freedom doing time.

Occasionally, there would be a shakedown that interfered with the schedule. That was when something would happen, a fight, maybe, or someone would manage to get high, and the guards would get suspicious and do a random shakedown looking for drugs, pills, knives, or other contraband. They'd tear up your cell from top to bottom—undo the bed, shake out your clothes, even turn your socks inside out. They'd check your mattress for holes or other signs of hidden things.

My cellmate was an older mom of three who was in for beating up her husband—she caught him having an affair and beat both him and the girlfriend pretty badly. She'd already been in the system for three years and was transferred over for some reason. Thankfully she was really nice, and because she'd already spent so much time behind bars, she knew how to thrive in prison and was happy to teach me. Not only did she teach me how to use the sink and toilet as a refrigerator, but she also taught me how to hang pictures on the wall with toothpaste. That was one of the things I'd noticed when I first came in. As I passed cells, I kept seeing these collages of photographs and handmade art decorating the cells. Now I knew how to do it! I hung up the photographs of the kids my mom had sent. I pasted most of them on my bunk, and a few favorites I put on the tiny slot window because my eyes would always be drawn there, looking out toward freedom.

She also taught me how to make "brownies" with Oreos from the commissary and saved milk from breakfast. And she showed me how to make deviled eggs with the eggs they'd serve us for breakfast.

I was so fortunate to have her in my cell. She helped me actually have a good time. We'd have facial and hair days using our Dial soap and products from the commissary. She took out the plaits I got in the pod, combed out my hair, and then put it in one long French braid. It felt so good to have someone comb out my hair!

We'd visualize, talk out loud about our dreams for how our lives would look once we got out. How we'd spend time with our kids and just enjoy the freedom.

As I've said before, humans can get used to just about anything, and I got used to this new life. I started to talk to the other ladies to learn what their stories were, like one woman who'd taken the rap for her kids. She was like a lady I'd met in the pod—that woman was in her late eighties! She'd taken the rap for her son after a drug bust and had been in the pod for ten years waiting to be transferred. She said she was prepared to die there. At first, she said she took the rap because she was old and wanted to give him a chance to live his life. But eventually she admitted he'd probably either end up dead or in prison, too, and she said, "Truth be told, I'm more at peace in here than out there."

Her story haunted me. All the stories I heard in the pod or at Templeman bothered me. Some of the people in there were completely innocent. Others not so much. I'd hear stories about how they witnessed killings and beatdowns, and how they lived in fear, often of the men in their lives who'd beat them up.

And I saw things that haunted me. Some of the women didn't care about being naked in front of each other. They'd undress in their cell and walk naked down to the showers. One of those women was so young! She'd pass by, and I'd see her naked skin all eaten up. When I asked what was wrong with her, I was told she had HIV and syphilis. She'd been a prostitute and was raped by a man with HIV. She killed him.

I was grouped in with the worst offenders—those in for heavy drug crimes and charges of murder or attempted murder—because of my original charge. Even after my charge was downgraded and my wristband had gone from red to orange, I was still included in the cell block with the most dangerous women in the prison. I was with people with diseases you could see, that showed up on their skin, and people with diseases you couldn't see, like bipolar disorder and schizophrenia. But I learned there really was no difference between them and me, someone with a schoolteacher mom and sergeant major daddy. I had to sit next to them and eat at the same table.

And while yes, I was still scared much of the time, the longer I was there, the more I realized that none of them were the monsters I originally thought them to be. They were people, just like me, who, because of whatever circumstances they wound up in, made choices that landed them in prison. Who was I to judge any of them?

My daddy was always telling me proverbs for as long as I knew him. *When you make your bed, you've got to lie in it*, was one he frequently said. I never really understood until I made my bed by not listening to him and my mom. And there I was surrounded by women lying in their own beds after making them—who, likewise, never really understood what they were doing when they tucked in their proverbial sheets. Sometimes, you are just in the wrong place at the wrong time. Accidents happen. It's when you *knowingly* go into the wrong place at the wrong time, when you ignore the warnings of others, that you have to face the consequences. It's a choice you make.

More Court

I continued to look forward to court days. Each time I went, it would be rescheduled, and the judge would tell me the date. So I knew when it was coming and was eager for each one. I could be freed at any time!

However, court was another catch-22. My parents had money to help me, but did I want them to spend it on getting my kids out of the foster care system in Louisiana, or did I want them to spend money on my attorney? As a mother, my choice was simple: they spent it fighting for custody of my children, so I had a public defender.

He was a young Caucasian man who had just gotten out of school. Tall, with glasses and spiky hair, he'd frequently tell me, "It's not looking good. You need to plea out. Otherwise, if they find you guilty, you'll get up to twenty-five years."

I couldn't do it, though. How could I plead guilty? I'd done nothing wrong!

When I was transferred to Templeman III, my daddy started coming to court. At that time, he was a sergeant major and would wear his dress greens with all the medals he'd earned from the military. He couldn't talk to me or hug me, but he would sit in the same courtroom I did and lend his silent support. He could, however, talk to the judge, and he did so every time after my hearings. They'd meet in the back of Judge Castillo's chambers. That was when my daddy learned that what the police had told me about Horace was true: he had a record. In fact, he'd been before that very same judge in that same courtroom before and had run off to Texas. Horace had an entire life we never knew about in New Orleans.

My daddy would also visit me in prison. Every time I'd hear those words, "You have a visitor," directed to me, I'd get so excited. I knew it was my daddy! The joy was almost too much to handle. He'd sit on the other side of a glass panel and speak to me through a phone. We'd have only fifteen minutes, which would feel like forever in a good way. He'd show me photos on his cell of the kids and update me on what he and my mom were doing to get custody of them and the process they were going through. They couldn't get custody right away because my parents lived in Texas, and the case was opened in Louisiana. The CPS in Louisiana had to contact the CPS in Texas and do house investigations first to make sure their house was sufficient. Then they had to interview everyone in the family—my mom, daddy, and brother. But at least I knew Shaniqua was still alive and the boys were OK.

CPS also wanted to interview my dad (my biological father), but he refused. He wanted nothing to do with any of my situation. He visited me one time, just once, when I was in prison. He told me he loved me, but when I asked if he could help me, he said no. He did special assignments for the White House! Surely there was someone he could call or something!

"I told you not to marry that man. You could have prevented all of this if you had listened to me," he said. "But you chose not to. I just came to lay eyes on you, to make sure you were OK. But you're responsible for what happens to you." He left soon after that, saying it was too painful to see me like that.

Meanwhile, there were multiple hearings regarding CPS and the boys and Shaniqua—about one every sixty to ninety days, depending on the backlog of cases, and it seemed there was always new evidence against me. Judge Castillo had a reputation for being the toughest judge on the docket, and true to his fame, he was not sympathetic to me.

At one point, when I was feeling desperate, he looked at me squarely and said, "I can't release you because you have no family here," meaning Louisiana. What I took from that was he thought I was better off in prison than free. Only later would I come to discover he was one of the hardest, and most racist, judges in the court.

Chapter 6
Angels behind Bars

That roommate was one of my guardian angels in prison. It was her and a guard named Sergeant Houston. She was a bright African American lady with dark black hair who had been at it for a while. She had a mouth full of braces that'd flash when she smiled at me.

"Little Red," she'd frequently say, "what did you do? You don't look like you should be here." She seemed like she was genuinely compassionate toward me, something that proved to be true when E came into the picture.

E was a woman who somehow got transferred into our block and immediately took an interest in me. Even though we were under surveillance twenty-four hours a day, there were some women who managed to have relationships with each other in there, though it wasn't allowed The'd say, "That's my husband," or "That's my wife." I was new to that game but didn't want any part of it.

E kept coming into my cell telling me she was going to get to me. She scared me, so I wound up telling Mama B.

"E won't leave me alone! What do I do about it?" I asked her.

"Leave it to me," Mama B said.

Unfortunately, Mama B handled it with fists. They got in a fight that was bad enough they both ended up in solitary confinement. E was released first. I don't know why. She was pretty well known, so maybe that had something to do with it. And she was still after me.

I wasn't sure what to do, but I did know it was true in prison: snitches get stitches, so I didn't want to tell any authority figure. I did confide in my cellmate, though.

"E's not going to leave you alone," she said. "We got to get you out of here."

I didn't know how that would be possible. Somehow, my cellmate got a private word in with Sergeant Houston. Nobody knew that she snitched, but it worked. I was transferred over to the federal side.

I knew God had saved me. His hand was in that process. He was the one who made sure I got the best cellmate possible: one who'd teach me to find ways to bring joy into my dreary days. He had put me in a cell block where I built a family: we prayed together, and I was protected in there. He protected me.

That protection continued on the federal side. The federal cells were much cleaner and better kept than the state ones in Templeman III, so there was that. And the guards seemed more experienced. But also, there was another guardian angel, Nadia.

There were two inmates per cell who shared one bunk set. Nadia ended up being my cellmate on that side. But in a real way, she also ended up being a type of mother. A prison mother, if you will, because when you're incarcerated, you need a family, and that family is usually built from whatever opportunities present themselves.

I learned a lot from Nadia. She built on what my first cellmate had taught me, like how to turn instant ramen noodles from a salty soup into an actual meal with hot dogs we'd remove from the baked beans. She showed me an even better way of making brownies by adding Snickers bars to the Oreos and milk. You'd mix it all together into a log and smash it with your sandal. I even learned how to make "Mexican soup" by putting pork rinds in the hot ramen soup water.

Deeply religious, she would get down on her knees every night and say a prayer while holding my hand. She also taught me about fasting. Nadia would read the Book of Psalms from beginning to end, and when you got to the end was when you would break your fast. We fasted for twenty-four hours, only eating fruit, to show penance, like Jesus in the desert, who fasted for forty days and nights. You fasted to show suffering while you prayed in hopes of God recognizing your good intentions and pain. So we fasted for Shaniqua; we fasted for my boys; we fasted for our release from prison.

During that time, Shaniqua started improving. In fact, she did so much better that my charges were downgraded. My red band was taken off, and an orange one was put on. The orange one meant "accessory after the fact." Nadia assured me it was because we'd prayed and fasted.

Nadia had been in for a long time on drug charges and for trafficking immigrants. She expected to die there because she had no papers and was stuck waiting for her country to pick her up—which they didn't seem interested in doing. She had long salt-and-pepper hair, and although only in her late fifties, maybe early sixties, you could see the weariness on her face. Because she'd been in there for a long time, I think about sixteen years by then, she had some privileges most others didn't because she worked in the laundry. Looking back, that was another way God provided for me in prison. We had extra towels, sheets, and blankets. She made sure I had more uniforms and somehow got me a set of pajamas and a whole bedspread with flowers on it! Our cell was the most decked out one—she even secured us some posterboard for our collages.

Her position also gave her access to the kitchen, so she kept us stocked with jalapeños and fresh fruit other than apples and oranges, like grapes.

She was Hispanic, Dominican, and would only speak Spanish, which probably helped us bond. Instead of calling me Little Red, she called me Chiquita. A lot of the people in the federal block called me that. On the state side, most of the prisoners were African American or Caucasian; on this side, most of them were Hispanic. I felt more at home there and let my Hispanic side come out. Perhaps helping that was when a Hispanic woman would come for services and bring her guitar.

There were no boisterous games of spades or dominos on that side. What card games did happen were far less energetic. I think that was because there were more readers over there, more sophisticated people in for things like money laundering, practicing nursing without a degree, and other former professionals. There was even one person, a white woman who was yet another person God provided for me. She knew what was needed for me to get a divorce.

Divorce

Throughout my time in prison, I wrote letters to my family, to Daniel, who remains a true friend, and to my old pastor from the church in El Paso. I let him know he was right: I'd gone into the wilderness. He kept up correspondence with me, as did many others from that church, encouraging me to keep faith and reminding me that God was watching over me, that He protects the ones he loves. They assured me I had to be where I was in an unknown land that was the wilderness because God loved me enough to put me in prison versus letting something terrible happen to me that would put me six feet underground (or above ground in Louisianna). Then one day that pastor wrote me saying God would release me if I got a divorce from Horace.

I didn't need any more encouragement—I just needed a lawyer. Or so I thought. But God brought me the next best thing: a friend I met on one of my numerous trips to court. She was a white woman in her mid-fifties, heavyset, with long blond hair and glasses. Several

of us would have hearings on the same day, and we'd go together on the bus. Sometimes, we'd strike up conversations to learn what we were in for. Court day was always full of hope and anticipation because our sentences could be shortened in an instant, and we could get a release date—sometimes that same day. So we'd root each other on and pray for each other's early release. We couldn't wait for court day.

When my new friend found out my story, she offered to write up a draft of the divorce papers.

"Can you do that?" I asked her. "Don't you have to be a lawyer or something?"

She laughed and explained she was in prison for practicing law without a license. She knew the law well enough and knew for sure in the state of Louisiana it was legal to handwrite your own divorce papers. She knew the legalese I'd need to make my divorce stick. All she asked for in payment was two packs of Oreo cookies, three Snickers bars, two packages of instant ramen noodles, and a bar of Dial soap. Easy!

That was how everything got started.

Horace had tried to contact me during this time, but the authorities still refused to allow us to speak to each other, so they sent his letters back to him. Each time we'd pass each other going to court, both with guards and in handcuffs, he'd profess to me he didn't do it. That he loved me and wanted me to hold on. That it was the devil, and we'd get through this. He continued to stare meaningfully at me when we were forced to be together before the judge, as if trying to convince me of his innocence with his gaze.

For my part, I didn't send Horace letters because I was still mad about what he'd done and the denial he still maintained. He fought the divorce, but the state of Louisiana doesn't require both parties to sign divorce paperwork. After a while without a response, the state automatically grants the filing partner a divorce. That was how I did it.

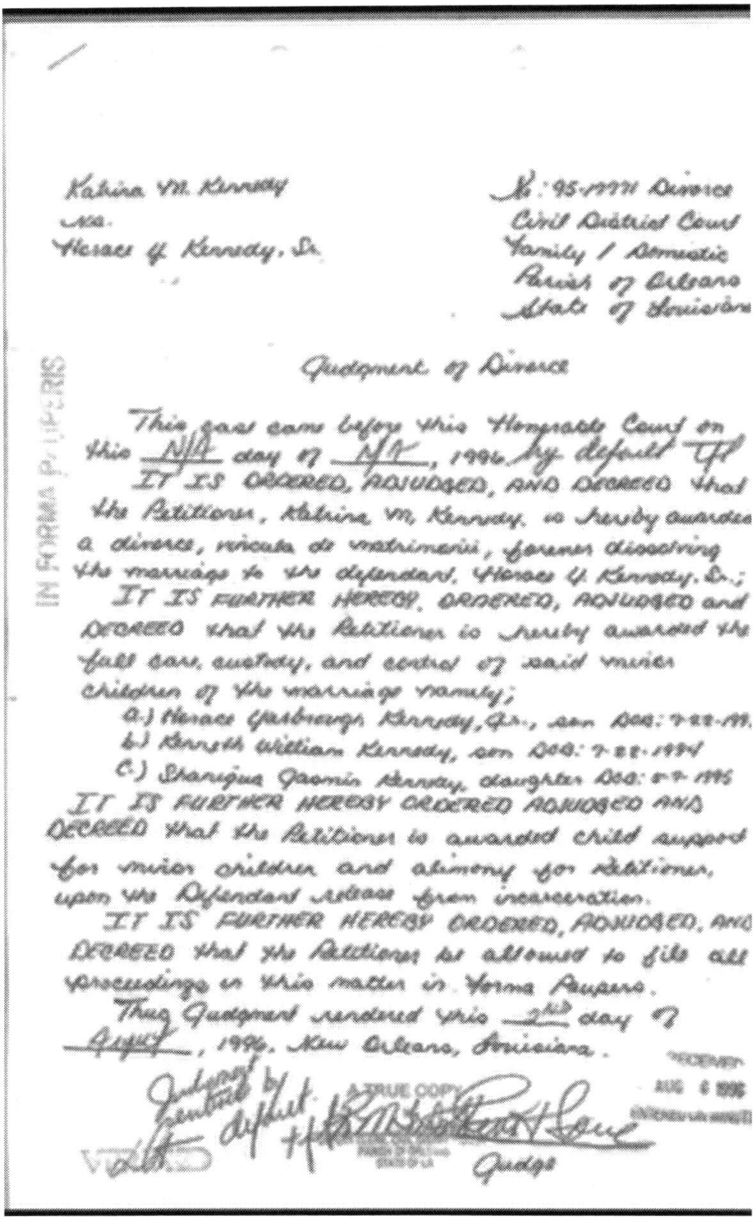

Katrina M. Kennedy
vs.
Horace G. Kennedy, Sr.

No: 95-[illegible] Divorce
Civil District Court
Family / Domestic
Parish of Orleans
State of Louisiana

IN FORMA PAUPERIS

Judgment of Divorce

This case came before this Honorable Court on this N/A day of N/A, 1996 by default [illegible]

IT IS ORDERED, ADJUDGED, AND DECREED that the Petitioner, Katrina M. Kennedy, is hereby awarded a divorce, vinculo de matrimonii, forever dissolving the marriage to the defendant, Horace G. Kennedy, Sr.;

IT IS FURTHER HEREBY ORDERED, ADJUDGED and DECREED that the Petitioner is hereby awarded the full care, custody, and control of said minor children of the marriage namely;

a.) Horace [illegible] Kennedy, Jr., son DOB: 7-22-19[illegible]
b.) Kenneth William Kennedy, son DOB: 7-22-1994
c.) Shaniqua [illegible] Kennedy, daughter DOB: 8-9-1995

IT IS FURTHER HEREBY ORDERED ADJUDGED AND DECREED that the Petitioner is awarded child support for minor children and alimony for Petitioner, upon the Defendant release from incarceration.

IT IS FURTHER HEREBY ORDERED, ADJUDGED, AND DECREED that the Petitioner be allowed to file all proceedings in this matter in Forma Pauperis.

Thus Judgment rendered this 2nd day of August, 1996, New Orleans, Louisiana.

A TRUE COPY

AUG 6 1996

Judge

My handwritten divorce paperwork.

His family wasn't in the picture at all. They'd all turned against me, thinking I'd done the harm to Shaniqua, that he was innocent, and that I should stop blaming him for my misdeeds. Later, I did reconnect with a few of them because I wanted the kids to know that side of their family, and some still follow me on social media and are amazed at how God has blessed me.

Relationships/Rebounds

The idea of divorce was freeing for me—at least as far as my marriage went. But that freedom only went so far. I also felt hopeless, the emotion that comes with prison and not knowing when you'll be able to walk past those bars for good.

I went through a period of doubt. I thought God had forsaken me. Forgotten about me. And even though I had some connections and a couple of older protectors, I still felt alone. I still wanted to be loved.

Many of the women would speak to the male prisoners through the toilets. They'd drain the water and use an empty toilet paper roll to project their voices. Nadia wouldn't let me do it, though I wanted to. But then I met a girl. Jocelyn was bright with short hair. She gave me the attention I didn't know I craved. I thought I was falling in love with her. She was the first woman I ever kissed romantically.

But my guardian angels knew such a relationship was the wrong thing for me. When Nadia found out, she looked at me incredulously. "Don't be stupid! What are you *doing*?" I'd been on that side for about six months by then, and she was solidified as my mother.

She cried, "Why would you do this? You are my daughter. You cannot let the flesh win! Your soul is more important to me, so you can't be in this cell anymore." To Nadia, following the edicts of the Bible was her first priority.

Next thing I knew, Sergeant Houston got wind of it. She transferred me back to the state side.

Men

They threw a welcome party for me when I returned to my old block. Mama B and Faith were both still there, as were many of the others who knew Little Red from before. They put on a full spread complete with chips from the commissary and deviled eggs made with pickle juice. It was the kind of thing they'd do for a birthday party.

This time, I entered feeling more confident. I had an orange band on my arm. My kids were with my parents by that point, and Shaniqua was going to be all right. I still didn't know when I'd ever get out, and I was feeling pretty lonely. I had a chat with God about it: "OK, so I can't be with a female, and yeah, I'm married, but hopefully not for long, Please. I'm human. Is there someone you can give me?"

The options were few, but I made do.

At that time, Templeman III had four different cell blocks. I was moved across the hall, to the cell block that had the men's cell block below us. That was where I learned I could finally talk to guys through the toilets. After the 7:00 p.m. roll call, we'd make a microphone of sorts out of empty toilet paper rolls jammed together to make a long tube: our microphone. Then we'd empty the water out of the toilet bowl, put our makeshift mic inside the hole, and spit: "Fffthuh, fffthuh!" With our ears to the toilet roll tube, we'd wait silently for a response. The soft noise would carry down the plumbing, and the guys at the bottom would hear and talk back, asking us to write to them.

Of course, we weren't allowed to communicate this way, and speaking loud could get us into trouble, but once we had a name or even a general direction, we could send a letter through the unofficial prison mail. We'd take our little eight-by-eleven notepad and get excited—we were talking to someone new, even if it was just through pen and paper.

When we went outside, we could pass a letter through a messenger, sometimes another inmate, sometimes a bribed prison guard. On our regular walk through the yard, we'd sometimes see the guys in their windows. They'd hold up a piece of paper with "Write me" or "Here's my number" in big black letters. If we knew a name, prison number, and cell number, we could send our letter directly through the prison's mail service. The whole process of communicating this way could take up hours and hours of time, but the effort was better than doing nothing but sitting with your own thoughts.

If you could make a regular connection with a guy, sometimes you'd become pen pals and share small stuff. Who we were. How much time we had left. Where we were from. We'd ask each other to share good food recipes or to be girlfriends or boyfriends. We'd say where we'd go on a date when we were out and work up to more intimate and explicit conversations, all through letters. It was all another type of fantasy, an escape from the reality of the cold metal confining us. We knew following up on any of this while incarcerated was next to impossible, but it was still cathartic. We were still free in our minds, and we could use our imaginations to fill the void for a little while.

For what it's worth, I never viewed any of the relationships I had in prison as serious. We were all just looking for a warm spot in the dark. We were all just passing time.

Passing Time

Passing time was my major occupation while in prison. While incarcerated, you have nothing to do *but* time. That's why they call it "doing time."

And you did have to do something within the limited options open because otherwise the thoughts in your head would eat at you like a beast in the dark, taking a bite out of you here, a bite out of you there, until there was nothing left.

I'd love it when the guards came in and said, "Mail is here!" and my name would be on the mail call list. We lived to hear our names get called. We lived through our letters. That was the only way we could track time from the outside, and it was another form of communication.

In addition to the letters from those male pen pals, sometimes I'd get a call or letter from home that gave me a tiny window into the outside world and soothed my worries about my kids. And of course, my daddy would sneak in one of his favorite sayings, like *freedom comes with a price...you've got to abide by the laws of the land...when you make your bed, you've got to lay in it.* The updates were brief, as calls were expensive and could only be fifteen minutes. The operator would come on when you had one minute left and give you a warning. I hated that one-minute warning, even though I was lucky in that my parents let me call them almost every day so I could keep track of their custody battle.

Like someone washed away in a flood clings to a fallen branch, I clung to whatever small bits of humanity I could get in the letters, calls, or occasional visit. But at one point, amid all that timelessness of a suspended life, I lost hope. I thought I'd been doing everything right. I didn't wear makeup. I went to church. I obeyed my husband—and I still landed in jail, with my boys in foster care and my daughter in the hospital. What had I done wrong? How had I sinned?

Sometimes, we'd see a prison chaplain when we attended scheduled church services held in the gym. Every week or two a different type of church leader would come in to talk about their version of the Lord, and you had a choice to go or not go. I never went to the Catholic ones, but if it was a Christian preacher or pastor from another denomination, I'd go. Sometimes, it wouldn't be a sermon at all, and we would just sing hymns or form a little prayer group that could sometimes fan the small flicker of faith we somehow held onto in all that darkness.

Maybe because of the different religious experiences I was having, I started reading the Bible through a new lens. Then, there was this one Hispanic lady with glasses and short hair who would bring her guitar and talk to us from a different level. She interpreted the Bible in a way that got me thinking differently about the scriptures than I had before. Nadia had already shown me her ways of interpreting the Bible, with her fasts connected to the Book of Psalms. This woman's messages were so different that when I'd be by myself, alone with my own thoughts, I'd start to hear voices, but not ones coming from the toilet. These were more divine. And they helped me learn the Bible for myself. She helped me interpret the Bible in a way that rang true to me.

When the Bible says your husband is supposed to love you like Christ loves the church, what does that mean? Does that mean Christ beats the church? Absolutely not.

What was David going through when he wrote the Book of Psalms, also called the Book of Prayers? "Yea, though I walk through the valley of the shadow of death, I will fear no evil" because the Lord walks with you. He walks with you through the wilderness. All I needed to do was learn to recognize it.

There was a lot of self-reflection, a lot of reading the Bible on my own, with no one to tell me what I should or should not take from it. Those study skills from my childhood bubbled up, and I was engrossed. I had time to ask myself the big questions that everyone faces at some point: why was I here? My mom was a teacher. My daddy was a sergeant-major. How did I end up in this situation?

At first, I was also trying to reconcile why God would choose to punish me for doing what I thought He wanted me to do.

But eventually, I realized maybe that wasn't it.

Maybe God had put in motion this awful thing because He saw it as my only way out. Maybe, if I wasn't in prison now, I'd be dead. Or my kids would be dead. Or my family.

That' was how I kept thinking. That was where my mind would go when feelings of despair and devastation creeped up on me.

I dreamed a lot about God back there behind the cell walls. I would ask, "Why are you taking me through this? What are you trying to show me? Why me?" And I'd find myself bargaining with God. "Oh, but if You let my baby live...if You let my parents get custody...if You show me this favor...I'll do this to serve You for the rest of my days and never disappoint you again."

I thought I was going to be as perfect as Jesus, and that was the goal I was supposed to meet to gain God's favor. But maybe we can't be perfect. Maybe that's the point. And striving to be as perfect as Jesus is another fantasy. How can we be that perfect when all we want is for Him to answer our prayers?

In time—all that slow, quiet time—I got acclimated to my life behind bars. And even in that dark, quiet place, God gave me what I needed: family.

Family

In Templeman III, the "family" structure was pretty simple. You had an adopted mom like Nadia, who was older and wiser about the ways of prison. You had an adopted dad, who was an especially butch woman. You had your sisters. And you just learned how to come together.

Many women didn't get money on their books so they could get commissary supplies. The adopted mother or father would make sure they could get those special treats that could make life a little more bearable. A candy bar, a cup of ramen noodles, a pair of socks. They made sure what they had, you had because you formed your own little family.

There was always a give and take, just like with any family. On grooming day, you'd ask someone to do your hair. We couldn't have sharp objects—long leg and armpit hair was a fact of life rather than a political statement—so usually grooming involved putting your hair up. I wore mine in one or two big braids. When the girls would ask me for a stamp or some paper to mail a letter, I'd give it to them.

I was nervous about my new cellmate after being separated from Nadia. You never know who you'll be sharing that tiny space with or what they've done. But I ended up becoming friends with my new cellmate. We couldn't really help it, being with each other almost 24/7 for an indeterminate length of time. We told each other secrets when the cell doors were shut and the guards called, "Lights out!" We became each other's sisters. Depending on experience and age difference, your cellmate could be more like a mother, like with Nadia, or an auntie.

My cellmate after Nadia was also older. Dark-skinned, salt-and-pepper hair braided down both sides of her head, heavyset. She was respected, in for heavy drugs, and no one messed with her, not even the guards.

The guards would give the rest of us trouble sometimes. During roll calls or when we had court dates, the guards would interact with us up close, otherwise they rarely came into the cell block. That was when they'd try to talk to us or make passes. I can't count the times I was propositioned for sex. All I knew how to do was keep my eyes down, act like I hadn't heard them, and make sure I didn't go anywhere in the prison alone. Because my daddy had visited enough, the security officials knew who he was, and his military ranking probably lent me some semblance of protection. Someone respectable would be told if I were harassed. But there was a limit to what they could do from the outside.

But the biggest protection came from my prison family. When the pressure for sex from the guards got too much for me, I told my Mama B about it.

"I'll handle it," she said simply.

I was never bothered by them again.

I don't know what Mama B did, but I do know she'd been in with the cartels, though I don't know which ones. What I learned later was that the cartels had some of the guards on pay to take special care of their loved ones. Mama B was one of them. In fact, she was so special she had a cell phone.

Due to her protection, I was never raped by a guard, nor by a female. Not even a lady who came on to me heavy after I told her I wasn't into girls. She was there waiting for her court date for setting her lover on fire.

While there may have been women who silently hated their roommates, for the most part, everyone in the prison formed a bond with the people they lived closest to. Prison is so lonely. So isolating from your family, friends, neighbors, coworkers—all the people you knew and who now may never talk to you again. For us, the cellmate was filling a void. A void left by a spouse, or boyfriend or girlfriend, or a child, a mother, someone we had loved and been loved by. When I returned to the first block, my cellmate and I would play dominoes and spades. I'd learned how to count my deck and was a beast at both games. We'd play for hours and hours. With no access to family or other friends, in your most dire moments, you turned to your cellmate instead. And if, for whatever reason, two people didn't get along, the guards would separate them and reassign one to a different cell or cell block, as happened to me. But sometimes, circumstances would make a girl a pariah, as I was horrified to witness when a new girl came in once.

Every so often, someone in the cell block would end up on the news. There was a girl, I forgot her name, but she was really young, around the same as me, just a teenager barely into womanhood. Her boyfriend burned her baby and the baby almost died. She had two small kids. When she got to the cell block, everyone was waiting for her.

I knew exactly how she felt. She was crying, saying, "I didn't do it! I didn't do it!" I just wanted to go to her. I wanted to say, "I'm in your shoes."

But before I could do that, the other girls had already gotten a hold of her. They thought she was the one who'd hurt her baby, and that's a crime the other women wouldn't forgive, so they made her life in prison torture. They would take her commissary when she would order food. They would make her perform oral sex on them. They would make her their fetch girl, "Do this!" or "Do that!" and create chores for her to do.

There's a power structure in prison, just like anywhere else, to keep people under control, and it doesn't just come from the guards.

If whatever you did ends up on the news and the news convicts you, they're ready for you when you get back there, to the pod or cell block. Whether you did it or not, they were ready for you. That part of the movies, at least, is real.

I had sympathy for her and what God was putting her through, but I can't say I didn't send a small prayer of thanks to God because my case had not ended up on the news. No one knew exactly what had happened with my daughter. Would they have done the same thing to me? I didn't know. All I knew for sure was that I had somehow been granted God's favor. I never got sick. I never got into a fight, though I got close to it before our family mothers intervened and saved us from solitary confinement.

God had His angels surround and protect me, and that new girl didn't have that kind of protection. In my small way, I would give clues to the girl that I knew what she was feeling. I knew the agony of her crime, and what had led up to it. I knew. And hopefully she understood, in this new onslaught of abuse, that she wasn't alone.

Eventually, months into my sentence, I felt comfortable enough with a few of the other women that I opened up a little and told my story. It always happened at night. The night before we went to court, it was common that we couldn't sleep. The anticipation of getting freed was too much. So in the dark, in that neverland between hope and despair, we confided in each other. Once upon a time, I had a good family. Then I made a bad choice that made the bed I now had to lay in. Choices have consequences, so now I was here.

"Don't worry, Little Red," they said, "They're gonna get that motherf*****!"

Maybe because of God's favor, or maybe because they now knew me, the girls were willing to take my side and encourage me. We were all in there for something bad, be it murder or assault or drugs or burglary, and if we didn't encourage each other, who would? If our cellmate didn't do it, who else was going to?

In the morning, going to court, it was, "Hey, Red, you're going home today!"

"Hey Red, can I have your stuff when you go home?"

"Hey Red, send me a letter!"

It was almost like we would try to speak freedom into existence.

But there was another side of court day that wasn't so supportive. I live by the Proverb "Be as wise as a serpent and harmless as a dove. Matthew 10:16" I never understood it until prison. People in prison will smile to your face and then be quick to stab you in the back. They'll play you just so they can steal from you or even rape you. That's real life. If you trust them with sensitive parts of your story or let them in on what you're doing that is against the rules, they'll keep your secret until there's a trial where, if they can trade that information to make your sentence longer but theirs lighter, they will. So you have to be wise, not play your full hand, and be a little sneaky and a little cautious about trusting people, like that snake. You want to preserve your skin. But on the other hand, while you're protecting yourself, you also don't want to go out of your way to harm others. You want to keep that peace, like the dove, and not let self-preservation give way to cruelty.

Even today, I can't shake this lesson, and it takes a lot for me to trust someone. I'm careful with my stories, and I test people. If I say my dog is blue, I don't want to hear that detail come around again to me by another channel. Then I know someone's been telling my story to others, and I can't trust them after that confidence is broken. I'm never sure if they have the best intentions.

This is what prison teaches us. The good and the bad, the loyalty and the betrayal.

Faith was my sister and my prayer partner when the cell block closed. Most nights, when lights went out and the guards retreated, she'd sing Walter Hawkins's old gospel song "He's that Kind of Friend" to encourage us. The lilting lyrics about Jesus walking with us through our trials would carry through the silent cell block and echo off all the cement and metal, the commissary now turned into an amphitheater.

It was always beautiful.

Part 3
The Cost of Freedom

Chapter 7
Going Home

Horace ended up getting released way before me. While our cases had been separated, we were still prevented from communication—no calls, no letters—due to the case. But every time we'd see each other in passing on our way to court, he'd tell me not to take a plea because "they couldn't prove anything."

I wasn't sure if I wanted to take a chance and trust him. At the time, I just wanted to get out. Whatever I had to promise in order to be released I was willing to promise.

As it turned out, just seven or eight months after our arrest, his case was dismissed. I couldn't believe it! He was right! How could anyone let that happen? How could God let that happen? I hadn't done anything wrong!

Lord, I prayed, *you know the truth. I don't understand it. How could Horace get out before me? Lord, you know what kind of monster he was to me and my kids! And you released him before me?* I cried myself to sleep that night in the cell in total disbelief.

I hoped, I prayed, I'd wake up from the nightmare and discover it was all a dream the next day. But no. I woke up behind bars, and he was a free man.

I started crying again, started praying again. *God! I don't get it!*

Finally, my cellmate said, "Little Red, it's OK. Trust me, everything happens for a reason. You keep your head up. You will be free one day."

It took me some time to recover. I stayed in my cell for a week, lamenting to God, crying, not wanting to be bothered. Then Pastor Claudia came to do a service at the end of the week, and I wanted to see her. I attended the service and went up to her afterward to tell her what had happened. She recommended I read the book of Ecclesiastes.

Of course, Pastor Claudia knew just what I needed. Not only was the book of Ecclesiastes interesting, but it was oh so very true for me. That book talks about how bad things happen to good people and good things happen to bad people. It can seem so unfair, but it explains there's a reason for it all in the end. And it mentions there is a season for everything—specifically, "a time to be born, and a time to die; a time to plant, and a time to pluck up what is planted." It assured me I was just going through a season, that there was a purpose behind me being there.

The day came when it was finally my turn to be given options. About four or five months after Horace was released, I went to court on the morning of August 2. As usual, I met with my attorney before being presented to the judge. He had news: the district attorney was willing to give me a deal. My attorney said if I decided to take it, I would go home that day.

However, if I decided not to take it, my case would be presented to a jury. If they found me guilty of accessory to child abuse, I could do up to another twenty years in prison. That was the price Louisiana exacted against mothers in its attempt to stem the tide of child abuse in the state. It was believed moms needed to be punished for "allowing" child abuse to happen.

Of course I was interested! Whatever the stipulations, I was interested!

Finally, I would be free! After one year and two weeks, I'd get to eat whatever food I wanted. I'd breathe in the fresh air outside of

Templeman III. I'd sleep on a soft mattress. And most important to me, I would hold and kiss my babies again.

Yes! I'd do whatever the judge said. I wanted to take the deal.

We went before the judge after the plea was drawn up. "I'm going to release you based on three stipulations," he said. "Five years' probation. You take parenting classes. And you get your GED." He paused and stared at me disapprovingly before continuing. "You will never get your children back. Your only hope now is to get your life in order enough to support yourself."

His words stabbed me like a knife in my heart. Tears fell out of my eyes. I'd never get my children back! My dearest hope was dashed, gone out the window. I closed my eyes against the tears and asked God to, please, one day allow me to get my kids back again. With my future in God's hands, I signed the plea on faith—faith that yes, my babies would be back with me again one day.

After the papers were signed, I wasn't freed immediately. Instead of walking out of the courthouse a free woman, I had to go back to a jail cell in the courthouse until it was time to be transported back to the prison. I'd be released from there. But that transport only happened once a day so the guards didn't have to make multiple trips.

Before being escorted back to the holding cell, I looked over at my daddy, who, as always, was there to support me. He nodded his head and, with the biggest smile, said, "I'll be waiting, baby girl."

Even though I wasn't quite free yet, I was excited I could tell my cell house family that I was finally being freed. It felt like the longest wait ever until I had a chance to say goodbye.

At transport time, we were all ushered into a little holding cell to wait for the guards. They loaded us all up to transport together, and we headed back. Everyone was there, rooting for me like they already knew I was getting out. Once again, I cried. There I was crying at the end of my prison sentence just as I had at the beginning, but these tears were tears of joy.

"I'm going home, y'all!" I yelled as soon as I walked in. Everyone came to hug me, and a release party was thrown together. I ran to my cell to get myself together, and my celly informed me that I had received some mail from the courthouse.

It was my divorce papers! My divorce had been finalized at last. I now had two kinds of freedom to celebrate: my release from prison and my release from Horace.

The party began with a full spread laid out. They cooked noodles with pork skins and cheese. We had pickled deviled eggs and my favorite dessert: brownies. We played some last rounds of dominos and spades. We hugged, and we talked about how we were an inspiration in each other's lives.

When the party ended, I headed to my cell to figure out what would happen next.

I gave everything away. *Here's my ramen noodles! Here's my Snickers bars and my Oreos!* I also gave away my blanket, my soap, my brush, my toothpaste, my uniforms, and my stationery. Even my toilet paper!

And that was when it happened: the guards finally came in and said the words I'd been dying to hear for over a year: "Kennedy! It's time to *roll out*!"

I ran around one last time to give more hugs and say thank you. I promised not to forget anyone. "I'll write you!" I said over and over.

I went through processing. Someone handed me all the belongings I went in with, the dress I'd worn to go to the hospital to see Shaniqua all those mornings ago. What had been so precious to me in prison was now just stuff I didn't want anything to do with. But hey, I wasn't complaining. I was ready to go.

A few minutes past midnight, the doors opened, and I walked out a free woman. I felt like Cinderella putting on the ballgown. Now, I was free to be whoever I really was.

Fresh Air

The first thing I did when I got out was kiss the ground. When I looked up, I saw my daddy's red Toyota 4Runner, and there he was, my daddy, standing there with his arms wide open. The second thing I did was dive into his arms, crying in disbelief. The day I never thought would come was finally here. My brother climbed out of the front seat to embrace me as well. But then, when I got in the car, to my surprise, there were Junior and Kenneth, with the biggest smiles on their faces.

Even though I'd cried so much you'd think I would have had no more tears to shed, they poured out of my eyes. My babies! I was with my babies again! I clung to them tightly. They looked the same as they had when I had left them except they were a little taller and a little chunkier.

Yes, the judge had told me I'd never be with them again. But by this time my parents had fought for and won custody of them. I wouldn't be able to live with them, but I'd be close by!

I had freedom. I had my babies. "Give me McDonald's!" was my next request. I felt like a princess again.

We got something to eat (those chicken nuggets and fries were the best—not to mention the hot mustard dipping sauce and the Sprite) and hit the road. We drove through darkness and stars for the whole eight hours back to El Paso. I was unable to sleep because all I wanted to do was catch up with my daddy.

Eventually, our talk quieted. But my mind wasn't ready to stop. I went into deep thought and started processing everything that I'd been through in such a short amount of time. As I got to really thinking and reevaluating everything, it hit me: all the conversations that I'd had with my family, everything I had done, the decisions I had made.

I began to understand that our mentality dictates our level of freedom. I was a prisoner in my first marriage, maybe in more ways than I ever was in a cell. I was only freed from there by going into an actual, physical prison.

"Freedom ain't free," my daddy told me when he would write me, and he reminded me again on the day I was released. He often passed on little nuggets of wisdom to me. Every time my daddy came to my court appearances, he'd say something to me, give me a riddle or a moral phrase before he left. He might not have given birth to me, but I considered him my number-one supporter. His stories might not have been happy or light or what others might consider encouraging, but he always talked with a purpose. His words often hit home. I was floundering in the dark wilderness while in prison, and his words helped me process what was happening to me.

"Baby girl, you made your bed; you're gonna have to lie in it."

"Baby girl, every bad choice comes with consequences."

On the day I was released from prison, it was: "Baby Girl, freedom ain't free."

I've thought about that phrase a lot over the years. No, freedom isn't free. I'd paid dearly for mine, in more ways than one. I thought I'd paid my price for it back then—in the time I did behind bars. And now my time, and decisions, were my own again. Prison gave me a big case of the "should've's": I should've listened to my mom. I should've gone to school. I should've gotten my degree. I should've, should've, should've.

Because I didn't listen to my parents, I suffered the consequences. Because I wanted to get married and be grown up before I was ready, I had to pay. Like the fictional Little Red Riding Hood, I'd disobeyed my mother and stepped off the path because of a sweet-talking wolf, and the wolf had devoured me and my family. Now would come my rebirth.

You see, it's easy to be trapped by the should've's. It's harder to switch to the mentality of *What am I going to do to change?* I didn't have the answer to that question yet, but I was willing to work on it.

When I started seeing mountains on the horizon, something it felt like I hadn't seen in years, my insides started leaping. So much had changed since the last time I saw them. My parents now had custody of all three of my babies. I was a single woman, not a married girl-woman.

I tried to breathe deeply to keep my nerves calm. But that became harder and harder the closer we got to home—the closer to seeing Shaniqua. What did she look like? I hadn't seen any recent photos of her. Was she small? Was she big? Did she look like she did before? Oh, how I ached to hold her. I couldn't wait to see her.

Home Sweet Home

We finally pulled into the driveway. I ran into the house and was immediately enveloped by the scent of a homemade breakfast. My mom greeted me with a big hug. Shaniqua was on the couch. Though tears blurred my vision, I could see she looked the same way she did when I had to leave her, just a tad bigger. Her hair was braided back, and she wore her onesie and was sucking her thumb.

When I had that last, sorrowful glimpse of her in the hospital, she had tubes and lines connected to her body everywhere. Thankfully, they were gone. She just had braces on her legs. I hugged her tight to me, and yes, more tears fell. She made it! She survived! I could see where the surgeons had placed the shunt in her skull. I rubbed her head and thanked God because she'd made it.

I didn't understand why she needed leg braces. My parents explained it was because she couldn't walk. She still needed a variety of help.

More tears came. These were not of joy. The weight of the responsibility of that tragic situation crushed me. If I had just left him, so many things would have been different, better. If I'd left him, my baby girl would be walking.

My mom urged me to eat. It was time to pick up the pieces and start anew in life, beginning with breakfast. She laid the table out with eggs, beans, grits, sausages, pancakes, biscuits, and orange juice. That was the best breakfast ever, and not just because it was good food made by my mom but because I ate with her, my daddy, my precious kids, and *mi tía* and *mi tío* from my childhood, the ones who helped raise me, as well as their son. I was with my family, the people who loved me most and whom I loved most.

Because I didn't have custody and I couldn't live in the same house as my children, I couldn't move back into my old bedroom. However, I could live close by. I moved into a studio apartment above my parents' detached garage. My daddy gave me his credit card to go shopping so that I could make it to my liking with my own décor. I remember going to Walmart and Garden Ridge to get comforters, pictures, bathroom towels and rugs, pots and pans, and everything else you could think of. When it was all said and done, my studio looked like one out of a magazine, and I felt so good on the inside. The freedom to express myself in my own place!

My kids resided with my parents in the main part of the house. So while I couldn't legally be their mama, I could at least see them every day.

My first day back, all I could do was love on them. Kenneth was now a chubby-cheeked two-year-old, and Junior was three. At first, Junior just stood and stared, like he didn't know what to do, but they both remembered me. I can't even express how happy that made me.

While I was ready to move on with my life, I didn't want to forget about being in prison and the people I'd met there. At least, not at first. Soon after moving back, I asked my mom for some stamps so I could mail some letters to them.

But my mom told me, "You just need to start all over again. That's not your life anymore. Those girls you met, those people, they aren't your real family. You already put your family through enough shame and embarrassment, and you can't go into this new life like that. You need to leave all that alone."

She made an uncomfortable point. I didn't want to be the person I was in prison. I'd grown some while I was in there, especially in terms of my faith. And I wanted to continue that growth. I had my own interpretation of the Bible now, my own ideas as to what scriptures were important and what they asked me to do. I needed to move on and leave my old prison family behind.

However, I didn't have a lot of friends in El Paso when I returned, the prodigal daughter. I still had a mess of aunts, uncles, and cousins, but aside from *mi tía* and *mi tío*, who rented my parents' basement apartment, most were standoffish. They knew I'd been somewhere. I'd catch the sideways glances and wonder what they were thinking about me. Or at least, that was my perception of them. They welcomed me back openly, but I couldn't shake the shame. I'd been the talk of the town. I'd embarrassed my mother. I'd disgraced my family. I hadn't listened, and now everything felt like a big "I told you so." I couldn't shake the idea that I was being judged from all quarters. That they thought I was guilty. It was a vision of myself that made its own kind of prison of fear that kept me always a step or so apart from all the others. The irony is that twenty-eight years later I discovered that my family never knew where I was at. My mom had kept that to herself to protect me and my kids.

Finding My Place

Moving back to El Paso was also strange in the sense that even though it was full of family and good memories, it was also full of the old burdens and people in my past who had, in some small ways, put me on my path into the wilderness. My cousin Julie was one such. I'd envied her when we were in middle school, with her new shoes, party-girl confidence, casual drug habit, and nonchalant attitude toward the rules. She was gorgeous, with her Hispanic sun-kissed skin and long, straight, black hair. Beautiful enough to be a stripper and make money with her looks, even as a teenager. She didn't seem like she wanted for anything. I'd wanted to be just like her, which was, of course, another source of tension between me and my mother.

In some ways, even after everything we'd both gone through since those carefree nights of sneaking away to frat parties, I was still in competition with her. Getting out of jail with nothing, I saw everything she had, all the material possessions, and wanted those things, too, just like before. Of course, this sort of covetousness, I now knew, came with a cost.

I reconnected with my cousin, and I still envied her, but I also had other priorities. I had to be a mother, even though my parents had custody until I could meet the judge's criteria before I could even attempt to fully step back into that role. I had to take parenting classes. I had to get my GED, which took about three months, my old study habits coming back like the proverbial riding of a bicycle. I had to do a lot of things to meet my parole requirements.

The authorities didn't think I'd be able to do it, but they didn't know me like my family knew me. They didn't know my determination, a determination allowed to emerge once again now that I wasn't trapped in the emotional chains of my first marriage.

My mom had my back, and she's one of the strongest people I know. She took charge in more ways than dictating my clean break from my prison life. By the time I was released, she'd already found a GED program through UTEP. I was signed up for parenting classes not long after enrolling at the college. Quickly, quicker than I would have been able to do on my own, I was on my way to meeting the judge's stipulations and getting my life in order. That was when my new journey started. This being the early 2000s, all my classes were in-person. Being by the border, the students were a mix of everything, all races and all ages.

I didn't want to go to my classes. They were all long and boring, the most flavorless servings of education you can get. And I didn't think I needed them. The only crime I'd committed was staying in a bad marriage. I wasn't sure what I was supposed to learn from this punishment. I also didn't follow advice to go to therapy because I didn't believe in therapy. I had my church to sustain me. What else did I need?

So getting my GED was filled with mixed emotions, especially when I was just slogging through what felt like a ton of busywork and tests with none of the social trappings and event milestones of high school. The "graduation" felt a bit out of time and place, just a small ceremony in the classroom where you got a piece of paper. I felt a small sense of accomplishment, a small amount of gratitude, but for the most part, I felt empty.

I had other things occupying my mind: a depression born from a lack of self-worth and shame that kept me apart from my classmates. I wondered if they knew of my past, as if there was a signpost I couldn't see with "ex-con" lit up like the Fourth of July with a big arrow pointed at me. I wondered if they knew who I really was. I wondered if they knew I'd gone to prison, if they'd still want to be around me. The self-doubt made me wonder if I was worthy to even be there.

Those thoughts extended outward from my small group of classmates. Once I had my GED and was better positioned to fill out job applications, I had to mark the checkbox next to "Have you been convicted of a felony?" Would these people even give my application a second look after seeing that, or would it go right in the trash? Just seeing the question would freak me out. It would take me back and make me remember that time in my life that was now a permanent part of my identity, to be re-litigated every time with each job application.

I wondered who would love me like this, a single mom with a record, no job, and three kids, one now disabled because I didn't leave. The thoughts whirlpooled around my shame of becoming the person my family had warned me I'd become if I didn't listen to them. Who would want me? Who would love me? Would I ever have a normal life? Would I ever be good enough? The longer I was out, the hazier being back there, in the jail, became. And what my mom had said eventually seemed the best advice: I did not write to my former cellmates.

Chapter 8
Seeing What's Possible

You never forget who was there for you in dire situations. Likewise, you never forget who wasn't, like the people you thought were close family or friends who scattered or ghosted you. They forget—or don't want to remember. I've since learned that doesn't just apply to stigmatized crises like prison.

I had a chance to run straight back to Daniel, my first love, when I got out. In fact, he and the crew were so happy to see me that they threw me a kickback like we used to have in the good old days prior to my getting married. One thing was different, though: I was more aware of my surroundings since I was on probation and couldn't afford for anything to go wrong.

The kickback was everything, though. There was meat on the grill, drinks everywhere, spades and dominos on the tables, trash talking, and, of course, some banging old-school music—Eazy-E, NWA, Public Enemy, and more. We were all still a big family. I was still part of it. I knew no one would mess with me—if you messed with one of us, you messed with all of us. It felt good to be around them. More than anything, it felt good not worrying about anyone looking at you crazy. Because they had also been to jail, I was accepted among them.

Daniel had begged me not to get married, but I did it anyway. However, he never turned his back on me. He was one of the few people who stuck by me through my first marriage. While I was behind bars, he'd written me letters and put money on my books. The Bible says that there is a friend who sticks closer than a brother (Proverbs 18:24). But while I could have reignited our romance from the past, something held me back. He was still a drug dealer, and I couldn't risk going back to jail for anybody, especially when I was fighting to get my kids back and rebuild my life. I loved him, but I didn't love him more than my babies. And he accepted that, which is why we're still friends to this day. My mom questioned me about that: "Is that the life you would have wanted?" But nothing she said could sway my affection. He never hurt me. He never forgot about me.

There's something to be said about loyalty. He could have turned his back on me when I went behind bars, but he didn't. He made it a point to keep in contact with me when I was at my lowest, and for that, I will be forever grateful. You see, people tend to forget about you when you no longer exist in their vicinity. So it says a lot about the ones who decide to stick by your side at your lowest time. Regardless, as much as I loved him and appreciated him for never turning his back on me, I knew that was not a life that I wanted or desired anymore.

Besides, I didn't have time for romance. I had to get to church.

After all my praying, I felt I owed God my loyalty for letting me go. So while I didn't rekindle my romantic relationship with Daniel, I did run back to Pastor Moore and the congregation I had known as a married woman. They had also stuck by me when I was in prison; from afar, they had helped me keep my faith and spirit up and provided that last boost to get my divorce. After all, the pastor's words came true: I was released from prison when my divorce was final!

I felt comfortable with them, though I wasn't sure how I'd feel entering the same church where I married Horace. Still, I couldn't wait to tell Superintendent Moore that he was right about my release, couldn't wait to be in some house of the Lord.

My mom still wasn't a fan of Bethel, despite my attempts to defend the congregation to her. I truly felt Superintendent Pastor Moore's words had played a big part in holding my faith, so I wanted to go back. Besides, by this time I was more knowledgeable about my faith, having done my own Bible studies away from Horace and his mother. I was surer of who I was and even felt comfortable stretching the rules here and there. I'd wear lipstick on occasion. Sometimes I'd even put on a pair of pants.

I was happy to discover my newfound perspective on what the Bible says was supported by my old congregation. They held up different examples of figures in the Bible going through similar trials to what I'd gone through. They assured me God must have loved me quite a bit to put me away, to save my life so they didn't have to attend a funeral and put me six feet underground. They told me it was all OK. That what I'd gone through was OK. That acceptance meant a lot. So I went back to where it all began, hoping to get the story right this time.

In fact, I found myself going back to church every time the doors would be opened. That was my way of letting God know how thankful I was for another chance. I became part of the choir and the usher board. Every time the prayer line would open, I would be right there asking for a special prayer for my children. Each time, I prayed that I'd get my kids back.

Transition

There was a brief moment of transition when I had to go back and forth to Louisiana until my case got transferred to Texas. My daddy had a niece by the name of Sheila who lived in New Orleans. I met her for the first time as I came out of the courthouse with my daddy. There she was: a beautiful light-skinned, thin lady with long black hair.

"Hi, Monique," she said. "I'm Sheila." She was already familiar with my story because my daddy had filled her in. I felt so intimidated because you could see success all over her. She headed toward a white Mercedes, opened a door, and looked at me. "Monique, get in."

I just stood there and stared. She said it again as she settled into her car. "Get in!"

So I got in.

My cousin Sheila was young and successful, working in the IT field. She was single and had no kids. She lived in a lovely contemporary studio apartment, decorated in pink and green.

"What do you do?" I asked, impressed.

"I'm an AKA, part of the Alpha Kappa Alpha sorority," she said cheerfully. "And just another slave of corporate America."

"How do you become an AKA?" Wheels started turning in my head with new hope after my release. If I could do something to set myself up, I would.

That hope was quickly dashed. "Oh, that's something you can never be because they only take the finest, and you have a record. You have to have a college degree." Which was something I obviously did not have. Her face sharpened, making her pretty cheekbones stand out among the carefully curated midcentury modern color scheme of her home.

OK, got it. I was a ninth-grade dropout. I was divorced. I had nothing, not even my kids. I might be free from the physical prison, but it would never let me go completely. I was now permanently marked, and others would see me only as an ex-con. I was nobody. She had everything a young girl could dream of: a good job, no kids, and a luxury apartment, and at the time, she was dating an athlete.

Every time we went somewhere together, she grabbed attention. She would be dressed to the nines, and of course she wore pearls with everything. She dressed in the finest labels, and she traveled everywhere. Believe it or not, she became one of my biggest inspirations because I would sit there and dream about what it would be like to have a life like hers, an apartment like hers, a car like hers, or clothes like hers (because she was such a good dresser). We did bond. We'd have some of the best girl talks at night, and she gave me some of her clothes.

Maybe that was why I let myself get involved with a police officer who used to flirt with me when I was in jail. He was an older guard who transported us back and forth to court. He was a tall, six-foot-one, bald-headed chocolate man with a whole lot of muscles and a goatee. He drove a black Cadillac with maroon seats and a sound system that was amazing.

In the early days of my freedom, when I was in Louisiana staying with Sheila, I'd go on dates with him, or he'd take me to his house to make dinner for me. He didn't tell me I was a nobody. He would always tell me how beautiful I was and how he didn't care that I had three kids. He always said the right things. He'd play Al Green every time we were together, the kind of music I listened to with my dad. It felt like a dream.

As Horace's wife and a good Pentecostal, I'd been forbidden to listen to the kind of music I'd loved before marrying him. I had missed Al Green.

I was still looking for acceptance and safety. Here was this mature police officer, with a house, a car, and a stable life, doing normal things. He knew I was an offender, that I had nothing, and he still wanted to be with me. At least, that was what I told myself at the time. Of course, later I'd realize he only wanted to sleep with me, but back then my self-worth was fragile, and I would have believed that anyone who told me they loved me only had good intentions for me.

Still, that little rebellious girl who lived inside me, who'd been pressed down into silence during my marriage, started opening her eyes. As she began getting used to the freedom of being able to think her own thoughts, she started making decisions that would turn her life around.

I wanted to show Sheila I could be somebody. I wanted to show them all. Especially since she introduced me to a life that I never knew existed. Even though she was in my life only for a brief period, she made such a huge impact.

One thing I have learned in this thing called life is you don't know anybody's story, even if you think you do. You'll never even know the half of it, even if they tell you the whole thing. Some of the girls I met in jail were innocent. Some sacrificed themselves for others. Some had mental health issues. And some were back there because they wanted to save their lives. We didn't live their story with them, so we can't understand why they did what they did or felt what they felt. And casting stones doesn't fix anything; it just lets you pretend you won't ever be the one getting hit. Everybody has a story, and stories always have two sides.

If I were to give myself one message at that moment in my life, standing before people who doubted me with a fragile new dream shattered, it would be: you can make it. You don't have to be a statistic. You don't have to remain in the belly of the beast. The wilderness has an end. And you can show them all.

After twenty-seven years, I finally saw my cousin again. It's funny how God allows things like that to happen. In April of 2023, I was at her aunt's house when she walked in. We made eye contact, and I asked, "Do you remember me?"

She did. When she said yes, I was able to greet her with, "Hi, Soror!" because I had become an AKA member. We hugged so tight with tears in both of our eyes. Who would have thought back then that when I saw her again, I'd be something she said I could never be? Her Soror! *Won't he do it!* (I'll explain in the chapters to come).

My Heartbeats

I fought for my kids, and I eventually got them back. I had to attend parenting classes once a week, sometimes twice a week. From the classes, I graduated to supervised visits.

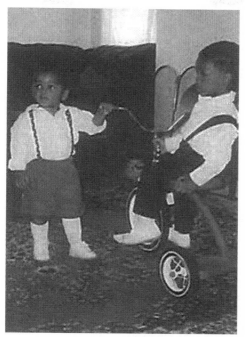

The boys when they were with my parents.

There were still several steps in the process that had to be done before I'd be able to get them back. Chief among them, I had to be able to provide financial stability for them; I had to get my life together and be able to support them. The amount and height of the hurdles made it almost impossible. However, I was up for the challenge. I got turned down left and right for jobs because I was on probation, and I had a record. Finally, after receiving my GED, I got brave, and when applying for a job as a bank teller, I decided not to check the box asking if I'd ever been convicted of a felony. I got the job! I didn't like it much, so I later found one as a customer service representative for a telephone company.

Little by little, piece by piece, things finally came together for me. I was able to be with my kids whenever I wanted since they were upstairs, and I had a laid-out studio that looked similar to the one Sheila had. My parents made sure that I was always well dressed, which was something that became important to my mom when she realized how low my self-esteem was. She wanted me to know what I liked, what I wanted, and to know I deserved to have it. I also enrolled in the University of Texas at El Paso (UTEP) to take some basic college courses.

I had my parents' car (a brand-new, pearl-white, sporty Chevy Cavalier), so I didn't need to go buy one. And I was able to take the boys out on dates and do things I had always yearned to do with them. Shaniqua, on the other hand, needed a little extra attention because of her disability, so I didn't take her out as much.

My parents hired a full-time nanny from Mexico to help with the kids. Her name was Soco, and she was probably in her early sixties at the time. Soco used to babysit one of my mom's students, and when that family no longer needed her services, she came to my mom to see if she knew of anyone who needed a nanny. To her surprise, my mom hired her on the spot. The day she moved in, Soco became an answered prayer (literally a gift sent from heaven). Another piece of my life coming together.

With the added support, I finally felt able to care for and protect my babies, which became increasingly important to me. After I was released from prison, I learned that while the boys were in foster care in Louisiana, they were never separated because they had stable relatives who wanted them; therefore, they were never in danger of being adopted.

Unfortunately, though, they still had to deal with foster parents until my parents were able to secure custody. And there were predators who took advantage of the situation. My boys were molested. I don't have all the details. It's hard to sort them out, especially since I was in prison at the time. But my parents told me later. After they got custody, my mom noticed they were protective of their bodies, especially when she gave them a bath. They really didn't want to take baths. Almost like they didn't want to be touched. And they would cry. They were only two and three years old, but she was able to put two and two together and found out they'd been molested.

It had taken much longer to get Shaniqua back into the family. She'd survived what her father had done to her but was left with cerebral palsy from the injuries. The family that took her in was good and wanted to adopt her. My parents met them and confirmed they were kind, loving people who would take good care of her. But she belonged with us, and my parents fought to keep us together. I will forever be indebted to my parents for this.

Even though I could not change what had already taken place, I was able to change the trajectory of how things panned out for me and my children in the future. I was beginning to slowly find my grounding.

Chapter 9
A New Chance at Love

I dated my second husband, William, for six months before we got married. While I don't remember how we met, his friend Warren does vividly and was able to fill in the details.

I met Warren at Fort Bliss. He approached me and expressed an interest in me, even when I told him he shouldn't be interested, and we struck up a light flirtation. One night, when we were talking on the phone while he and William were at a baseball game, he passed the phone over to William. William and I clicked immediately. We ended up talking all night. The next day, we connected in person, and I asked him if he wanted to go to church with me that following Friday. Pastor Moore always said we'd know our future husbands if they went to church with us on a Friday night. William met me there that night, and we went out to eat at Golden Corral when the services were over.

After all my struggles with self-worth, William seemed like a gift. He had a son up in north Texas, so he was already OK with fatherhood, and he seemed to like me and my kids. He was also a military man, so I knew he had a steady, respectable job, and I was very familiar with that lifestyle. I thought I was following in my mom's footsteps and that this time I'd found a good man. But I guess

I didn't think all the way through to the places where my mother's footsteps had led her.

I thought I'd paid the price for my freedom and was on my way to happier times. What I didn't know was that the wilderness wasn't quite done with me yet, and God still had some lessons for me to learn about what being free, and free to love myself, really meant. Meanwhile, there was William. So handsome with his chocolate skin and beautiful smile. His teeth were so pearly white that you could see them from a mile away. He drove a loaded blue Honda with silver rims and a nice sound system. And he was such a gentleman! He would open the door for me and always compliment me on how I looked. He treated me well. We'd go out to dinner at nicer restaurants than I was used to, and he would always pay.

Perhaps most impressive, he was fine with being an instant father of four, and he didn't mind taking the boys to get haircuts or providing for me and the kids. He would even love on Shaniqua! He didn't care that she had a disability. With that charming and accepting personality and great career, he was like a cross between both of my fathers. He was perfect.

William also loved me for me. As I mentioned, I'd started to bend the church rules a little, even though church was still a center point in my life. I wore pants more frequently and even used lip gloss and lip liner to accentuate my lips. William told me my lips were beautiful, that they were one of the features he found most attractive about me. That affirmation silenced those old childhood taunts of Big Lips. William liked them the way they were. It was an affirmation that I was attractive and lovable. That was what made me fall even harder for him.

And when my love for him led me to open up about my past, he accepted that too. I was still closed off from most people, still living under the assumption that people didn't like me, that they feared me, and that I wasn't good enough to be around them.

Granted, my pastors had tried to combat that narrative. They told me God had something special planned for me. "You know who you are," they'd say. "Don't settle for less. Take your time." But even with their constant encouragement, I felt like shame and doubt hung over me like a cloud. I couldn't believe them. I did know who I was: a single mother with a record and on probation. My soul felt hollowed out by all my mistakes. I was trapped in my own mind, even though I was free in my body. I'd sometimes think, *Am I really free at all?* And I'd fear if I didn't follow the path in front of me, would I ever get another chance at love and a stable life?

William had broken through my cloud of doubt with his bright, flashing smile. I felt like a princess again, this time living the rags-to-riches story of Cinderella. So I ran to my prince, partly out of relief and joy and partly out of desperation because I never thought that someone would love me and my kids.

As we got to learn about and know each other, I found out that he also was the main provider for his sisters and family in Vernon, Texas. Every time they called and a bill needed to be paid or they needed money, he would just take care of it. This did something to me. You see, my daddy took care of a lot of people, too, so I couldn't help but think that I'd met someone just like him. Again, something I didn't think all the way through.

I introduced him to my parents a couple of weeks after we started dating. William said the Lord told him I was going to be his wife. He would also quote scripture to me. Especially Proverbs 18:22: "He that findeth a wife findeth a good thing." I thought God was letting me know He'd sent William to find me. Quite honestly, that was a turn-on. He was doing all the right things. I felt like this was a confirmation from God that he was the next husband I'd submit to as a wife. Yes, those are old-school religious beliefs, but they were mine at the time, things I believed to my core. William didn't have a regular church when I met him. Therefore, he ended up becoming a member of Bethel as well.

Four months after that, we were married by Elder Eugene at Bethel (the same church that my ex-husband and I were married in). It was a very small and intimate wedding. The only ones in attendance were his mom, his sisters, his aunt, his son, my sons, my mom, my brother, and, of course, my daddy. After we were married, we went to a restaurant to eat. Six months doesn't seem that long to date for some people, but he was doing all the right things, and remember, I was only twenty-two years old.

While my stepdad, being military himself, was fine with me marrying a military man who had a stable career and loved me and my kids, my mom wasn't so sure. She had formed a poor opinion of all men in uniform. In fact, she thought they were dogs. Never at home and always sleeping around. But then again, she had said more than once that a man will always be a man; as long as he takes care of home, that's all that matters. Of course, she was going off her own experiences, which I didn't think could apply to the whole species. Besides, I was sure she was wrong about this one. He loved my kids. He went to church. He had a respectable career. His family came up from Vernon, and after meeting them, it was like we belonged together, so all I could think was, *Please, let her be wrong about this one.*

Moving to Vernon

Shortly after we got married, William ended up getting out of the military. As soon as he was discharged, we moved to his hometown of Vernon, about an eight-hour drive from El Paso. He had a job waiting for him there, working for the city. Vernon was also where his firstborn lived along with his whole family: his sisters, mom, granny, uncle, and auntie.

The idea of separation didn't sit well with my parents after my first marriage took me to New Orleans and what happened there. He reassured them he'd take us home for visits, and they saw how William loved my kids, had an honest living, and was remaining within the state, so they were willing to give us their blessing.

We packed up the Honda, and off we went: William, me, and my boys. Unfortunately, Shaniqua had to stay with my parents. Her cerebral palsy, caused by her skull fracture and the subsequent brain damage, had paralyzed her left side. She couldn't talk or communicate in a substantial way, and she needed assistance with all daily tasks. My daddy told me that when she was on life support in the hospital, he asked God to allow her to make it. He promised to take care of her if God would only let her live, and he was happy to support her high needs. Additionally, my parents were extremely overprotective of her and the boys, and since she couldn't talk, they wouldn't even consider her going anywhere. So she stayed with them, where Soco was her constant companion, helping her twenty-four hours a day. While my heart broke to leave her behind, I knew she was in the best place, since I couldn't give my daughter that level of stability and care after another big move. And I knew she'd be up to visit us during spring and summer breaks.

Vernon is a small country town that sits close to the Oklahoma border, north of Dallas, just outside Wichita Falls. It's a funny little town. Very segregated, which was new for me. We lived with William's aunt and his two sisters, who were very young, close in age to my sons, in a nice, three-bedroom house that I could decorate the way I wanted. The boys thrived with their new family. I found a new church about an hour away in Wichita Falls (High Praise Church), so I was able to stay with the same religion. I started wearing only dresses again to fit in with my new congregation and their firmer ideas of holiness, and the familiarity of their rules felt like home to me. We counted our blessings. It was a new beginning and a blank slate.

I got a job as a unit secretary at the local hospital, and William worked for the city. No one knew my past. I'd taken a chance once again and hadn't checked the box next to the question about past convictions. I just knew if I did, I'd never get hired anywhere that promised an actual career.

At first, I'd monitor and answer the call lights of the patients and answer the telephone, directing callers where they needed to go. Then, I was trained in how to be a telemonitor and watch the telemetry machine. Literally, I watched the heartbeat of the hospital.

I ended up getting certified as a tele monitor tech, and then, having mastered physicians' atrocious handwriting, I became a nursing assistant. I even flirted with the idea of becoming a registered nurse. But that was a dream best left unpursued since I later learned you can't be a nurse if you have a felony conviction.

I bonded with a coworker named Toya. She didn't have any kids, so mine balanced the equation between us. It was nice to have regular, adult conversations with a friend.

And I felt important. Prestigious. I was helping to save lives. Some might think my actual job had a small impact, but to me, the job was everything.

Yes! My life was really coming together. The boys were enrolled in school, and when they weren't in school, they would attend the Boys and Girls Club. There wasn't much to do in Vernon, so to pass time, we would stay home playing dominos or spades, and on weekends we would head to the flats (a park where people went to drink and hang out). Vernon is where I was first introduced to blues music. Cecil Mae (William's aunt) loved listening to Johnny Taylor. "These Last Two Dollars" was one of her favorite songs. She also loved to highside (trash talk), so you can only imagine that we never had a dull moment.

I was even introduced to new-to-me foods: pig feet, chitlins, pig ears, Kool-Aid pickles, greens, and black-eyed peas. Then there was Cecil Mae's favorite I'd never heard of and was scared to taste: she loved her neckbones! Especially with greens and cornbread.

It was such a fun adventure! Even the kids enjoyed getting accustomed to their new lifestyle. They quickly bonded with William's sisters and their new stepbrother, playing outside together until the lights came on. They grew so tight. When one got into trouble, they all got in trouble.

It was all so perfect! We even went to church every Sunday. When we didn't drive all the way to Wichita Falls, we would go to the neighborhood Baptist church. I couldn't ask for a better life.

But then, shortly after moving to Vernon, William's mom passed away. That was the first funeral I had ever attended. And poor William! He was so hurt; it didn't seem like he'd ever recover. In fact, he did a whole 360 after we lost her. We started arguing over the smallest things. And he wasn't as engaged as he was before with his family. In fact, he pretty much shut everything and everyone out except for his granny. That one who had his whole heart. I couldn't help but wonder where the man who I had married was.

Then one day I went round to his granny's house. That wasn't unusual. She frequently needed something taken care of in her house, so we'd go over every week to check on her. But this particular day, while she was rocking back and forth in her rocking chair, crocheting and chewing tobacco, she casually said, "When God taketh, he giveth another."

I wasn't sure how to respond, so I waited a beat. Then out of nowhere, she said it again.

Wouldn't you know it? That was when we found out that I was pregnant with Janae.

The smile on William's face was priceless when I told him. It was the first smile since his mother had passed. We ended up finding a three-bedroom pink house on the other side of the tracks and moved into it shortly. He let me decorate it however I wanted, and we went all over the area buying new furniture. Soon after, we bought another car: a maroon Chevy Camaro that was fully loaded. A new car, new house (to me), and new furniture. What more could a girl ask for? I was in heaven.

Making things even better, my brother Tony lived nearby. He had moved to Vernon, too, to be near me again, and was working at a youth correctional facility. He got a house of his own only about eight minutes up the road from ours.

Tony, my first ride-or-die!

Men Will Be Men

Even though William's mood lifted a little with the news of Janae, he didn't reconnect with me right away. He would stay out late at night. He wouldn't communicate, and his patience was low. Most of the time, I felt as if I was just there, some person in the same house as him. His phone stayed on silent when he was home too. It got me suspicious. I began to suspect he was cheating on me, but when I asked him about it, he denied it.

However, we weren't really sleeping together anymore. He also had quit going to church with me. I told a church elder of my suspicions. I told her I thought my husband was having an affair. Her advice: pour holy oil in his shoes and rub his naked back with the oil whenever we were intimate. I did it. I guess it was supposed to keep him loyal, but there are some things God (or holy oil) can't fix.

Soon after, I went to work, where my friend Toya told me her sister was pregnant and that the father was my husband! My heart dropped. I couldn't believe it. I went to my boss and told her I needed to leave due to an unexpected emergency. She let me go, and I raced out of there.

Since Vernon is such a small town, it only took me about five minutes to get to him, but those five minutes seemed like five hours. With tears in my eyes and so many thoughts going through my head, I remember calling my mom and telling her that I was about to pack up and come home. My intuition was true. He really was having an affair. Why couldn't it be with someone else? Why did it have to be with my only friend's sister? I didn't get it. I knew my life was too good to be true.

As soon as I pulled up where he was working, he came and greeted me. "Hey, baby."

There was no calming me down. I immediately started yelling at him. "How could you do this to me? What have I done to deserve this? All I do is make sure you and the kids are taken care of! I cook; I clean; I go to work and go to church!"

At that moment he knew that I knew. His eyes filled up with tears. He hugged me tight. "I'm so sorry. It was a mistake. I never meant to hurt you."

He knew I wanted to leave, but he begged me to stay. That night when we got to the house, you could hear a pin drop. Things were so tense even the kids knew that something wasn't right.

We tried to talk. To me, I had been the perfect wife, but to him I wasn't the same person that he married. And I understood. When we met, we would listen to Keith Sweat, SWV, and other great music. I wore makeup, and I dressed to the nines. Now, I dressed like an old lady. I felt like I couldn't go anywhere because I feared I'd go to hell if I was anywhere other than church.

I had to question things. Could it be my fault that William ended up in the arms of another woman? Or was this just the way men were, and they blamed it on us?

My daddy, for all his good qualities, was unfaithful to my mom. Starting early on in their marriage, I saw different women coming to the house when she wasn't there. He was just like my biological father in that way.

Why did my mom let that happen? Looking back, I can assume she thought it was part of her sacrifice for her kids and grandkids. She was willing to trade stability and safety for security. The house was clean, gorgeous, and none of us went without food or basic necessities. My daddy took care of us like we were his own children.

So I thought cheating was normal. While I was angry and hurt, while I did want to leave, I stayed. I tried to believe it wouldn't happen again. I'm not sure I ever convinced myself, but disloyalty seemed like a constant theme in my life. Maybe people didn't need to be faithful to still have love between them.

From the Country to the City

Janae ended up arriving early. The day she was born, William was the happiest person in the world and more determined than ever to have his family together. We had moved on from the affair. We started going back to church as a family on Sundays, Tuesdays, and Fridays. Then the days that William worked late, I would go with just the kids. We had family night, and we would also go out to eat weekly. Life was finally normal again.

Toya's sister, who also worked at the hospital as a nurse's aide, had a baby boy a few months after I had Janae. I found out she'd gone into labor when I was at work. After my shift, I walked downstairs to the maternity ward and asked her point blank, "Is this William's baby?"

She stared at me for a few seconds before slowly answering, "That's a question you need to ask him."

Immediately, my stomach knotted up because in my heart I knew that was his child despite him saying that it wasn't. I went home and called my mom. But she wasn't much help in this situation. In fact, the call only reminded me, once more, that I grew up watching her keep going back to my biological father and stepdad after women they'd had affairs with came knocking on her door. That was the model I saw repeatedly growing up, so I let myself fall into line and repeated the cycle. As if adultery was the one commandment you could break without repercussions—if you were a man.

Again, humans can get used to a lot of indignities if they get enough practice. That was why I kept going back to my first husband, and it was why I went back to my second each time I discovered he was cheating. And at least my second loved my kids, including Shaniqua when we saw her on our visits home, and he was a great father to Janae as well.

At least there was that.

All military men are dogs, my mother would reiterate. But that didn't mean the constant adultery didn't affect me. My ego took a hit. I went back to the same old thoughts that plagued me as a teenager and prisoner: *I must be ugly. No one wants me. I'm damaged goods.*

William began reinforcing this narrative. Maybe it was his guilty conscience making him act out—I'm not sure—but he started giving me some choice words as well. He didn't hit me physically, but words can deal just as big a blow. "I don't come home because all you do is nag," he'd say when I tried asking about his affairs.

I wanted to understand. Was it me? How'd we get here? I went to church. I was faithful. I did all the things a loving wife was supposed to do. I cooked. I cleaned. I was there to help support him and his sisters. What else did he want from me? I'd thought he was the perfect person for me, sent from God, and to know I'd chosen poorly again—chosen a playboy who couldn't stop loving women—didn't feel good. In fact, I thought everyone blamed me for being stupid and mishandling my relationship.

We tried separating for a time. But then William called and said he wanted us to move with him to Dallas, where he could make a better living and support all his kids. "I want my family," he said. "Let's start all over again in this new city." I was willing to try. I couldn't stand living in the tiny fishbowl of Vernon anymore, where everyone knew everyone else's business and the affair was practically public knowledge.

So we moved to Dallas. He went first to get established. While he was there, I made friends with William's best friend's sister, Sabrina. We grew close. Really close. My relationship with Toya was strained at this point, to say the least, as Toya didn't want to get in the middle of a love triangle, so I had no one to talk to about it. Sabrina listened. And I had a lot to tell her. But I began to suspect that my new best friend was also a little too close to my wayward husband.

We eventually joined William in Dallas in a three-bedroom apartment in the suburb of Duncanville. I got a new job as a title expert at the Dallas Auto Auction right down the street, and William worked at William's Rent-a-Center as a manager. Again, no one knew me or my past. I started going to a different church, still a Pentecostal one, but a totally new congregation.

At first, it did seem like we were starting all over again fresh. Things went well. Our apartment was nice. We were living on cloud nine.

But it didn't take long for me to come back down to Earth. *Lord to behold, here we go again.*

There was always a string of women pawning for William's attention. My best friend. His boss. Others who came knocking on my door in a weird echo of my mother's life. I felt a little paranoid, and when I confronted the women, they all told me I was crazy, but I couldn't shake the doubt or suspicion.

The one that hurt the most was Sabrina. She was supposed to be my best friend. The person I told all my secrets to. The person I unloaded on about William. And there they were, messing around behind my back.

When I couldn't hold back and would confront him, William increased the meanness of his offense. "Who's gonna want you?" he'd sneer. "You have four kids, and one of them's disabled. You were in prison. You're nothing. You'll always be nothing. Who's gonna want that?" Then he'd stomp off to the bedroom and watch TV.

Because he was ripping open old wounds, it was too easy to believe him. Because he was acting just like my daddy, it was too easy to see this as the rest of my life—me and the kids in one room, him in the other. The only one he'd pay attention to was Janae.

We didn't even do anything together as a family on the weekends anymore. He'd stay in the room and sleep all day, and I'd go off to church. We were stuck in a downward spiral. Eventually, even William saw it.

"You can leave," he said at one point. "But you're not taking my baby." I think Janae was his main concern all along, and the reason I'd tried to stick it out. I knew he'd make good on his promise to fight me tooth and nail for custody, even as he shut out the rest of us.

William's mom, whom he'd been very close to, was now gone, and his baby girl was his world, a part of his mom she'd left behind. She'd been born on the heels of her grandmother's death, and he fully believed in his grandmother's commentary that "when God taketh, he giveth." He didn't want to lose the last part of his mother all over again.

Meanwhile, the women kept knocking. William grew more distant. And I couldn't take it. I just couldn't take it anymore, so I decided to move out.

We separated again.

Jamasa

My boys and I stayed in Dallas and moved in with a friend I'd met at the church that I was attending. We were both part of the praise team and the choir. Jamasa was a revelation. She was three years older than me and had three kids around the same ages as mine. I'd made frequent visits to her house so that the kids could play together. She bent the rules to her liking, in service to her own confidence, and she passed her lessons on to her newest student.

"Hey, girl, put on some makeup. It's OK!" she'd say and teach me how to apply it.

"Hey, girl, let's dress you up—in pants!" she'd laugh.

"Hey, girl, you need to do something to this pretty hair." She'd comb my hair and sit me down and style my curls.

"Let's get you doing something," she encouraged, trying to build up my spirits. "Let's get you living for you."

"Let's get you to affirming," she'd say with a laugh.

"Affirming? What's affirming?" I asked.

"Come on, girl! I'm about to show you some things."

That was when I learned how to encourage myself. Telling myself, *I am beautiful. I am kind. I am smart. I can have whatever I say.* In other words, I didn't need a Prince Charming to tell me or provide for me.

She taught me how to start loving myself. We spent most of our time together at her house. Even though she was going through the same situation as me in that her husband had cheated on her and had a baby with another woman. She was trying to work things out with him, but she still found a way to be there for me and share her nuggets with me. We both ended up taking the focus off our husbands and putting it all into raising our kids. Friday nights would be lit at her house—learning to love ourselves and be strong.

We'd listen to secular music like Erykah Badu and India Arie while making soul food in her kitchen. We'd dance to beats, drink wine, and talk about regular things. Simple things. James (her husband) would just shake his head and go into his music room. He was definitely unbothered by our foolishness.

Soon I started to believe that I was beautiful, unstoppable, and powerful. I started to put more effort into myself and discovered a life I thought I could get used to.

Jamasa eventually left the church completely and formed her own personal relationship with God, but that was years down the line. To this day we are still closer than ever. The kids never skipped a beat either, and they call themselves cousins when they keep in contact.

On Our Own

I ended up moving to Grand Prairie. I moved with nothing but our clothes (by choice). By this time my brother was back in El Paso. I asked him to come to Dallas to help me since William and I decided on separating. Because he is his sister's keeper and she needed help, he came.

I found a job with the electric company and worked a lot of time to furnish our home (without the help of a man). And I did. I did something that I never thought I could do.

We started out with one TV and a few blankets, and we sat and slept on the floor of our small apartment. There was one week when we ate nothing but beans and eggs or ramen noodles. Christmas would get delayed that year until my tax return came in. But we had peace of mind. Nobody was yelling. Nobody was angry or sad or afraid. The peace both inside and outside of us was priceless. It was then that I realized the lesson I hadn't understood in my youth: money isn't everything.

We finally had our own place.

Eventually, I was able to add a chair here, a bed there, either bought at a discount or rented. I learned about resources for single mothers and that I could take the boys to the Boys and Girls Club after school and for summer programs for less than ten dollars a day.

I built a sanctuary for us, little by little, the way I wanted it. And I did it all on my own. Eventually, our sanctuary would grow into an empire.

It was like God had granted me superpowers, and I only now realized I had them. It was around this time that the name Monique no longer seemed to fit me anymore, and I started going by my first name, Katrina.

My brother lived in the apartment with us for a while. He'd come and go, and while he was there, he'd help. It was nice to be there for each other under normal circumstances.

I started believing in myself. Believing I could do anything. I proved the adage true: "She started to believe who she was meant to be, and the game changed."

However, the pull of William was still strong. Eventually, we decided to see each other, as we both missed each other. Once more, things were going great. I would go to his apartment; he would come to mine. We made it a point to date, have family dates, and go to church again. We talked about all the affairs and decided that we were just going to start all over again. We each had keys to each other's apartment as we were starting to build trust again.

One day, after the kids got out of school, I dropped them off with my brother and went over to William's place. I burned some candles, threw on some Erykah Badu, and started cooking dinner—one of his favorites (fried cabbage, smothered pork chops, and rice). I heard a knock at the door. He hadn't made it home yet, so I was skeptical about answering it, but I did. Why did I do that?

Of course, there was a woman looking for William because he had not been answering her calls. She proceeded to tell me how they had been dating for months; she was in love with him, and she was expecting his baby. I just looked at her and said, "OK. Well, William and I are going to get back together again. I'm not going anywhere." She started crying. I wasn't sure what else to do, so I closed the door and went back to cooking.

I was shocked by the conversation. Stunned. So I decided to call my mom, as usual. She heard me out and just let me vent.

Maybe she was hoping for something better for me. Or maybe she thought she had to believe in me before I'd believe in myself. Finally, she interrupted and said, "Monica, where is your dignity?"

I couldn't answer.

"I never wanted you to live like this," she continued. "To go through what I went through. I never wanted you to think this was

OK." Her voice softened, "You're better than these women. You're stronger than me. You're going to be OK. You don't have to stay." Her final words were a plea, almost a prayer: "Please. Please, don't be like me."

At that moment I felt something bust inside of me. The chains of a generational curse I hadn't even been aware of until that moment broke off and left me feeling lighter. Freer.

She was right. She was right!

This wasn't normal. I wasn't supposed to do this. A leopard can't change his spots, and expecting him to was folly.

This wasn't me. And I could do something different. I could support myself and my kids on my own. It might hurt, but I'd bounce back. That night, after that conversation with my mom, I finished cooking dinner, cleaned the house, wrote him a letter, and left for the last time. I finally chose me.

You see, when we separated, I left with only my and the boys' clothes and the Camaro. There I was, starting all over again, but this time everything that would be built would be built by me. Though William kept his word to my daddy and made sure that we were straight financially.

Building an Empire

I ended up filing for divorce. We'd been married for five years at that point, and the divorce process took a year and a half. This time, I paid for a real attorney, and it cost more than just ramen noodles and candy bars.

Even during the divorce proceedings, William and I tried work it out, but it just wasn't happening. One reason is because my mother's dignity question kept playing in my head. If he hadn't loved me enough to remain faithful when we were together, it wasn't going to happen now. I had finally put on my big girl pants and realized I needed to love me more.

I fought for Janae, but William wasn't having it. We ended up settling when it came to her. We had joint custody of her; however, he was the sole provider. I didn't want to take the chance of the continued reminders and recriminations of my past that I feared he'd throw in my face. I couldn't relive it all again. Therefore, I didn't fight as hard, which to this day is one of my biggest regrets.

Kenneth and Janae

I continued to work on me and on building a good life for my boys. I couldn't afford daycare, so to spend time with them, I'd keep them up with me at night. In our new normal life, Junior and Kenneth acted like typical kids of seven and eight. I had them both in sports, which Kenneth loved, but Junior preferred to clomp around in my heels. They got along well, but as with most siblings, they'd fight with each other and make messes, which caused me to fuss at them sometimes after coming home from a long day at work with dinner and football practice still to do. But they were good kids overall, charismatic kids, and we had some fun times.

My daddy would help us out a little here and there, but for my mom, it was important I make it on my own. Which I understood.

Shaniqua was still living with my parents. I'd make the long drive home once or twice a year, or my parents would visit, and I'd get to see her. Truthfully, I didn't make any special effort to reunite with my daughter when we were in Vernon and Dallas. It wasn't because I was ashamed of her disabilities, but I still lived under the idea that no one would want us if a child with special needs came with the package. And I still thought someone wanting us—me—was important. I'd found part of myself, but I wasn't all the way there yet. That skin was still new and tender. I still wanted to be loved, not as a daughter or mother but for only me. I wanted to be enough. Some might think that's a selfish or horrid thought, but then, I'm guessing some people didn't live through the same things I did.

After my divorce, my focus was only on building a life for me and my kids. I didn't date. I was probably a little gun-shy at that point. But eventually, I thought, *What's the harm?*

My first boyfriend, when I was ready, was another Kenneth. A big guy who loved me and the kids. But he moved too fast, and it scared me. I was technically still married, as the divorce wasn't final, and I didn't relish the idea that I'd somehow be committing adultery. Also, I'd had a partial hysterectomy while I was with William, so I couldn't give Kenneth any more kids even if I wanted to, and he didn't have any of his own. I called off the relationship before it ever really started.

It was maybe the first time I used my hard-won judgment to end a relationship. I was a little sad; he was a good guy, but it was the wrong time for both of us.

I also changed my denomination. I realized there was only one God and that religion is just religion. And the religion I'd been keeping to was stricter and demanding more than I wanted to deal with. The people in that church were very judgmental and opinionated. I just wanted to follow the Bible, not their particular interpretation of it. So I looked into nondenominational Christian churches. I still wanted to keep my faith in God and go to church, but I also wanted to decide what I would wear and listen to. I saw Bishop Jakes preaching on TV from the Potter's House and found out his church was in Dallas. "You know what?" I said to myself. "Let me go visit this church."

I was a little nervous walking in for the first time, but there were women wearing pants—even some people in sweatpants! And the place was huge! No one came up to me wanting to know my business. The service only lasted two hours, maybe three, and what he preached was like nothing I'd heard before. For one thing, his sermon was positive. Every time I heard Bishop Jakes preach; it was about ways to better yourself. "God's going to give you the vision, but you have to go out and work for it too," was a common theme. "What are you going to do to achieve your prayers?"

This was a total 180 from what I was used to. "God's going to bless you with a house," I'd hear from the other church. How am I going to get this house? "He's just going to give it to you if you believe in Him enough. If you have faith and follow these rules."

The thing is, I'd tried that kind of faith, and it hadn't worked out for me so well.

With this new church, the focus was on *your own actions*, which was the message and guidance I needed.

I never really believed in therapy, which is something a lot of people ask me about when they hear my story. And maybe this is because it was never part of my world growing up. Nobody I knew went to therapy, and they'd gone through similar experiences. We just talked to God and each other. I always figured God would be my counselor, and I'd use His words in the Bible to guide me on what to do next and how to grow.

My big lesson, culminating at this moment in time, was simple: if my husband couldn't show me dignity, I'd have to claim it for myself. Come Hell or high water, I was in control of my own life.

Maybe that was the lesson God was trying to teach me all along. The only path out of the wilderness is the one you make yourself.

That was the beginning of my transformation, when I finally stepped into the light. It's funny because now William and I are good friends. He's been over to the house to spend the holidays with us, and we have found a way to move past the hurt that we caused each other. I keep in touch with his sisters, and when Cecil Mae was living, she was still a deep part of my life. Life is short, and I'm thankful that we no longer let our past define our future.

Part 4
A New Season

Chapter 10
A Time to Flourish

My transformation and divorce coincided with my brother's wedding to Jamasa's sister in Desoto, Texas.

Tony had never put down his role as my protector, even after my first divorce and release from prison. When he was staying with me in Grand Prairie, Jamasa had come over one day with her sister Lisa. Tony and Lisa made eye contact, and a few months later they were married. It was a lovely wedding. But what made it especially lovely was the saxophone player in the band, who, coincidentally enough, also played at The Potter's House, the big church I was now a member of, though I didn't know the connection at the time.

There was my brother's bride, Lisa, in her gorgeous gown. It was one of the biggest moments in my brother's life. Serenading her with the saxophone as she walked down the aisle was a sexy saxophone player dressed in a fine suit. Jamasa caught me eyeing him up and laughed. "Girl, look the other way! You don't want to date a musician!"

Oh, but I could date this one.

Her caution was slightly contradictory since part of the reason the saxophone player was there was so they could hook him up with Jamasa's other sister.

I was dating Big Kenneth at the time and had brought him to the wedding. He could be an intimidating figure, to say the least. He was six foot three, dark chocolate, and very built (when he wasn't working, he was at the gym). I also had the boys with me at the wedding. Later I learned the sax player had started asking around about me but halted his inquiries when he saw me feeding my date, assuming I was off the market (and what five-foot-seven musician wants to compete with a dude that looks like a linebacker?). There was no way he was going to approach me.

But I couldn't stay away. I learned the sax player, Derrick, was going through a divorce the same as I was. We exchanged phone numbers and talked for hours, giggling like we were back in high school again. We decided to connect at a park the next day, and the following day, we decided to go to Pappadeaux Seafood Kitchen for dinner. Soon we were taking midnight rides to go get fish in South Dallas off Martin Luther King Boulevard at a tiny place called Catfish Smith. He'd go to my sons' games. And at night, silently enjoying each other's company, we'd listen to music for hours. "Sarah Smile," "Hotel California," "I'm Your Puppet," and songs by Rose Royce, Al Green, and Marvin Gaye made up our nostalgic playlist. Even some Garth Brooks and Reba McIntyre, popular in El Paso, made it in. Hearing those tunes again jolted me back to my carefree childhood, when I'd listen to that music with my dad. But he didn't just keep me in my musical past. Derrick and I also loved contemporary artists, some of whom Jamasa had introduced me to, like Erykah Badu, D. Angelo, India Aire, and Maxwell.

Music seemed to encourage me to embrace my self-worth, to fully allow myself to transform into the strong, independent woman I was destined to be. To this day, when I hear "Tyrone" by Erykah Badu, the lyrics make an impact. I understand more than most about being tired of a man's Sugar Honey Iced Tea. Or when India Arie professes we all must love ourselves—shaved or unshaved legs, combed or uncombed hair, and everything in between. Those songs were part of the soundtrack supporting me finding myself, continually affirming the message "You're good. You don't have to put up with anybody's stuff. You're gonna be all right. Don't worry about living up to someone else's standards. If you feel good about it, you do you."

And there was Derrick in the middle of it all. It was a true connection, a friendship built from joy instead of duty or flattery or the need for stability. I had a steady income rolling in that was decent. I had just purchased a new 2002 pearl-white Mitsubishi Galant. I was my own person, and he was his, and that was all we wanted from each other: our true selves. He was also perfect with the boys. He would take them to get haircuts and pick them up from the after-school program if I wasn't able to. He would take them to practice. I mean, he was just perfect.

But I was a little scared of perfect. We dated on and off for two and a half years, dancing around each other and each trying to reconcile our old relationships. Both of us would try going back to our previous relationships, only to find the same problems there that had triggered divorce in the first place. We had broken up a few times and gotten back together, but that last time we broke it off, I decided to move on. I ended up meeting a guy by the name of Sean. He was six foot four, bald-headed, with a goatee. He had a little belly on him, but he was still pretty buff. He drove an SUV and had his own place. He was another one who didn't have any kids. He was amazing with the boys and had a great job. We had talked about marriage, but I was hesitant because I couldn't have any kids, and he hadn't met Shaniqua yet. I expressed my concern to him, but he didn't care. Me and Sean were together for at least six months. Then one day while Sean was at work, Derrick showed up at my house.

I answered the door. I didn't realize how much I had missed him until I saw him again. Butterflies started in my stomach. He opened his sweet mouth, and the first words that came out were: "I really missed you."

I missed him too. However, by this time I had already moved on. He asked if he could come in; I let him. We picked up right where we had left off. That next day, after realizing that I never got over Derrick, I went to Sean's house to break it off with him. He didn't understand and refused to go out without a fight. He expressed his love for me and the kids and said that he wasn't going to let me go that easily, but my mind was already made up. He was a good man. Truth be told, any woman would be lucky to have him. I just couldn't do him like that. So I left and never looked back. Not knowing what the future held for me and Derrick, I decided to just go with the flow.

When we decided to get back together, we both wondered why we were wasting any more time. If we really wanted to be together, why not make it official?

One answer to that was I had a hard time trusting this picture. It looked too good to be true. He seemed too perfect. I checked in with my mom and daddy. They loved Derrick. They loved how he loved my kids. All my kids.

But then Derrick said something that made me question things even more. As we were talking about and making the decision to become one family, he said, "You need to get your daughter."

What? That was hard to trust. I worried he'd change his mind and leave after learning about all the extra commitment involved with Shaniqua, who was still living with my parents in El Paso. Yes, I wanted her with me. But I knew that if I wound up by myself again, I would not be able to provide her with the same quality of life my parents could. Did I want to risk upsetting her life that much?

"What about your music?" I asked him, testing his resolve, something I'd never been brave enough to do with any man. "You're well known. How do you feel about this? Truly?"

He grew serious. "When I marry you," he affirmed, "I'm marrying all your kids. All of them. They become mine, no matter their needs."

A sense of relief washed over me, an emotion I hadn't even known I was waiting to express, like I'd been holding my breath for years and finally let go. That made me fall for Derrick even more, if that was even possible. It chiseled away at the doubt I'd wrapped myself in since my first and second divorces.

Junior, however, at just nine years old, still questioned Derrick's commitment. He was standoffish at first, maybe because he didn't trust Derrick after our on-again, off-again relationship. However, his brother, Kenneth, advocated for him, and Derrick slowly built a bond with them all. By the time we were married, they called him Dad.

Junior's reluctance may have stemmed from something else. He was older now but still felt more comfortable in heels than in a football jersey. It was getting harder to explain it away as just a phase or believe he'd "toughen up." My religious beliefs may have broadened by this time to include pants and secular music, but I still believed, along with the church, that homosexuality was an abomination. That it wasn't what God intended. And Derrick, also a member of the same church, believed the same. I'd later come to accept Junior for who he was, but that was far into the future.

By inches, we all learned Derrick was exactly who he said he was. We even went through premarital counseling offered by the church, as by this time I was more open to talking through the past hurts, especially at Derrick's urging. There was a lot of healing I needed to do—both of us needed to do, coming out of our prior relationships. We may have been friends, but trust issues had led to the on-and-off pattern, and we didn't want to keep repeating that after we were married.

Counseling helped me trust that Derrick was sincere when he said he loved my kids like they were his own. After all the broken promises and abuse of my previous marriages, I had a hard time accepting that I could be loved as a single mom with four kids, especially since one of them was struggling with his own emotional issues and sexuality and one had disabilities that required around-the-clock care. It would be wonderful if the storybooks on full acceptance of a ready-made, imperfect family were true most of the time, but I'd found it was a rare partner who wanted the whole package, warts and all.

I'd survived my childhood. I'd survived abuse of all kinds and the wilderness my tolerance of the abuse had thrown me into. I'd survived OPP (Orleans Parish Prison) and probation. I'd gotten my kids back. I'd earned an independent life and learned to stick up for myself. I'd found a more supportive church and a more supportive man. Why should I still be in bondage over an old, exploitative idea of love? I'd survived everything to get here; there must be a reason for it. Didn't I also deserve to know what real, healthy love felt like?

Doesn't the sinner deserve redemption? A third act to get it right?

Finally, at this point in my life, I believed I did.

Third Time's a Charm

Derrick was a father of two girls. By this time, he was bringing them around so that we could start blending our families together. All the kids got along as if they had known each other since day one. Our weekends consisted of football games and church. Then after church, we would always go out to eat. Finally, he asked my parents for my hand in marriage, and they gave their blessings. Not long after that, the wedding planning began. My third wedding was huge. It was a fairy-tale wedding, and this time my prince would not turn into a big bad wolf. We'd seen each other for who we were before getting engaged and done the work with time and counseling, and we had our eyes wide open to reality.

We got married on the Top of the Cliff, a high-rise right outside of downtown Dallas that overlooked the sparkling skyline of the city. We had a big fancy cake, waiters, a DJ, and a band and singers. My kids were all there, as well as my whole family from El Paso. Derrick's best men were his brother, my brother, his best friend, one of his other friends, and of course the boys. As funny as it was, my new husband's first child's mother, Cressy, was my maid of honor. My attendants were rounded out by Shaniqua; my next-door neighbor, Roseio, who lived in the apartments at Fox Chase with me; Florence, a good girlfriend who was an AKA and would always tell me, "You can do whatever you want to do"; and another person whose name now escapes me (I kept telling my kids weddings are for other people, which means there will be at least a few people in a big wedding party you'll hardly talk to afterward). DK (Derrick's daughter) and Janae were my flower girls, of course.

Derrick played his saxophone while I walked down the aisle on the arm of my mom, who gave me away.

It was everything we wanted it to be, not the idealized princess wedding of a teenager, nor the quick elopement of a woman accepting what she could get. This was an adult wedding, a wedding fit for a queen.

We honeymooned in San Antonio, a first for me. We stayed in a hotel on the River Walk and drank the city's famous margaritas. Texas is known for its margaritas, which are everywhere, but these were high-class. Homemade sour mix and everything. We were in hog heaven.

When we returned home to Dallas, we started looking for a nice house to rent that could hold all of us, including seven-year-old Shaniqua and her grandmotherly nanny, Soco, who wouldn't be separated from her. By this point, CPS was long out of my life, and it was an informal handover of care from my parents. Shaniqua was old enough and communicative enough now that she'd expressed she was ready and excited to move into a household with her mother, brothers, and new father. This was a hard one for my parents, especially my daddy because he didn't want her to leave, but he understood that her place was with her mother and brothers.

We found a nice two-story, four-bedroom, two-and-a-half-bath house in the Dallas-Fort Worth metroplex. Life was blissfully normal. I'd almost forgotten what that was like. Soco would cook and clean alongside her duties as Shaniqua's support. She was like the Alice to our Brady Bunch. So after work, all I had to do was take the kids to football practice, get them bathed and done with homework, and spend time with Shaniqua in the evening hours when Soco was off watching her *novelas* (soap operas). We'd watch movies, and we'd talk about how our days went, an activity that was new to me. Someone was interested in my day! And on Sunday mornings, we'd go to church.

I was still with the electric company but transitioned to Aetna because it was closer to home, and I worked in their call center right up the street.

We could have settled in and become another family living the typical American Dream and average life. We were happy, after all. But a funny thing happens when you start discovering your self-worth: you start learning to dream bigger, to want to reach new heights. You trust that you can keep expanding in good ways. Eventually, we ended up building a two-story house but stayed in the Dallas suburbs. I was able to pick out every detail, which I loved. We bought a new black Cadillac CTS and a Ford Expedition. Life was great. While our house was being built, we ended up putting furniture on layaway so that we could pay on it monthly, and after the house was done, not only did we move into a brand-new house, but we also had brand-new furniture in every room. The kids didn't go without, and at this point we were one big happy family. We started traveling and doing things that I had seen on TV. We took all the kids on a cruise, and the rest is history! I could get used to this. At least twice a year, we'd drive home so that my parents could see the kids and so I could just go home. I ended up getting a promotion at Aetna, but I still was not content. I felt like something was missing, and I also felt like there was more to this thing called life.

There's Gotta Be More

My new church paved the way to new possibilities. I'd long dropped the simple idea that faith was all you needed to have a good life. I still had faith in God, but I was still working on developing faith in me. I wanted a better-paying job, but with a GED as my highest educational level, I didn't think I could ever do better.

However, in the sermons I now heard were new questions that prodded me to develop a new perspective. *Who says you're not enough? Who says you can't go back to school? Why are you doubting yourself?*

My self-doubt was a holdover from my past relationships, which I'd been giving way too much credence to. The Bible said to love your wife as Christ loved the church. Christ didn't beat the church or talk crazy to it. He didn't say, "You're not this," or "You're not that." No, Christ was more than a conqueror; he gave his life for the church. That was real love.

The Bible says to do all good things. It says I am enough because that's how God made me. Fearfully and wonderfully made. And as one of God's wonders, I would not be a passive statistic—I just had to do the work.

I had to take steps of my own, under my own power, to get to where I wanted to be.

Looking around me, I realized I was supported not just by God but by many. Derrick was one of my biggest supporters. My mom, of course, had been my cheering section since I'd first dropped out of high school. They planted the seeds of college, something, as an adult and an ninth-grade dropout with a GED, I thought was beyond my ability. They knew better.

The church had come out with a God's Leading Ladies program, built to bring out the best in whoever was part of it. The curriculum was based around women, to teach them how to be leaders in their communities. That was where I met Christy, a Caucasian lady, youthful, with blue eyes, and gorgeous. She had it all. We were study partners in GLL. And after seeing what I was capable of, she pushed me to go back to school. "You could be so much more," she'd say. "I see you going back to school. Why don't you?"

When your parents and husband encourage you, that's expected. But when a stranger sees something positive in you, who thinks you're not done living and have more to offer to the world, that's something else entirely.

Eventually, I thought, *If I don't go back to school now, then when is the perfect time to do anything?*

Meanwhile, Soco became sick. We took her to the hospital in Parkland, where the doctors diagnosed her with pneumonia and said she had little chance of recovery. Soco asked us to take her back to her homeland so she could pass there. We did, and Soco passed a few months after. Two years later, Derrick's oldest daughter came to live with us. In short, I had a very full house that needed a lot of attention.

But these new challenges wouldn't deter me from the path I was now set on.

I enrolled in Northwood University, a local school that made sense with my full-time adult schedule with work and family. I could take classes at night, with some additional Saturday classes that lasted all day. After I put my kids to bed and my husband was asleep, in a weird echo of my mother, I'd stay up through the midnight hours studying and doing homework. It was a sacrificial season in my life to complete my education, but I knew what awaited me on the other side.

I met new school angels. Katrina started her own educational journey at the same time I did. We got our bachelor's degrees together in business administration, a degree I could use practically anywhere.

I walked for my graduation. Out of all the fairy tales I'd woven for myself over the years, this one seemed the most fantastical. I couldn't believe it. Here I was, a ninth-grade dropout with a felony who'd been told time and time again she was a walking statistic, now walking across a stage, wearing a cap and gown, to shake hands with the university's elite and get her degree. I'd done it. I really had. I could show my kids you could make it, whatever the cards stacked against you.

I gave my mom my diploma. All she'd wanted me to do since I was born was go to school and get the education she'd been denied at first. That was all she ever wanted for me. I'd ended up being more like her than I'd ever imagined, especially as a rebellious teenager, but her faith in me had finally paid off. When I walked off the stage, it gave me joy to hand her the piece of paper that represented my degree in front of the family, who'd shown up for my moment of triumph. "Here, Mom," I said. "This is yours."

At that moment, I knew anything was possible for me if I believed it.

I threw myself the biggest graduation party ever. Rented out a restaurant, had a band play, and asked them to sing Marvin Sapp's gospel song "Never Would Have Made It." We partied until the lights came on for closing.

The Dream Becomes Reality

After I graduated in 2010, Christy pounced. Now the CEO of Integrity Transitional Hospital, a major hospital in North Texas, she'd been waiting for me. "OK, you're ready," she affirmed. "Get your resume together so you can come and work for me as a physician's liaison." She knew my felony record and didn't care. As CEO, she had the power to ignore that checkbox.

She gave me a job making the most money I'd ever made in my life. It was an amazing salary, plus bonuses! Another dream had come true! No, a dream that hadn't even floated through my wildest imagination came true: after chasing financial stability by way of others all my life, now I was the one who would pave the streets with gold.

Even then, I wasn't done. I'd tasted the top and knew I could go higher. I felt like I needed more. So I called Katrina, and we went back to school for a master's degree in business at Texas Women's University in 2012. There, we met our third partner in crime when it came to education: Chocka. The long nights, tears, and sacrifice were worth it! We did it!

One more thing. Years later, I was training in the gym and had met some ladies through my trainer. We all worked out together three to four days a week at 5:00 a.m. After two years of developing a relationship, we had a conversation, of all places, on the treadmill. This was when one of them told me that she was in a sorority. When I asked which one, "Alpha Kappa Alpha sorority," dropped casually from her lips.

"Oh," I said, just as casually. "I've always wanted to be an AKA member."

She asked me what was stopping me from becoming one, and I told her that I didn't know where to even begin. Shortly after, she started tracking my progress. She let me know that her chapter was getting ready to open a line and that I should apply. My mouth dropped. By this time, it had been over twenty-five years since my incident in Louisiana. Before I knew it, I had a sponsor to write a letter on my behalf to nominate me to the grad chapter.

I'm not sure what was sweeter: getting my master's or being invited to be AKA after receiving it.

Everything that man said I could not do—everything that judge in Louisiana said I could not achieve—I'd now done.

I even bought my dream car, a Range Rover. I walked into my purpose and drove that SUV straight off the showroom floor.

Katrina has finally arrived. Katrina feels very grateful and thankful. Katrina can't believe it, and sometimes she feels she's living in a dream, but it's here, and it's real. Even if the rug gets pulled out from beneath my feet, like so many times before, I'll see it for what it is: the season I'm called to live in. Whatever that season might be, bring it sun or rain or storm. There's a time for every purpose under heaven.

In those seasons, I learned to value myself, not let others define my value. This led to the dominoes falling in my favor. Good things came to me because I finally thought I was worth the good things. I knew now I could get them on my own, and I could concentrate on the characteristics I wanted in partners and friends and jobs. I could now recognize what was truly important to happiness.

In not needing, I got what I wanted. The dream finally became reality.

Chapter 11
Making Peace with Our Stories

I need to backtrack a little bit to a time when my first son, Junior, just kept giving me a hard time. It started shortly after he turned eleven. In the heat of arguments, he'd spit out his reasoning for his rebellion: "I give you a hard time because I want to know who my real father is. Where's my dad? Kenneth and I go to school, and everyone thinks we're bastards because we don't know our real father."

His words bothered me. A lot.

So I hired a private detective to find Horace. After the divorce, he'd cut all contact with us. And while it may be hard for others to understand, in spite of the past abuse, Junior still wanted a relationship with his biological father. The old traumas were now almost a decade past and fuzzy in his mind. Now all he felt was the void of his real dad.

The detective found Horace in Baton Rouge, Louisiana. We talked on the phone first. My nerves were everywhere, but I made it through the conversation. I went to see him, to talk to him about his son. I was nervous. Scared. Of course I would be. The last time I'd seen Horace was when we were crossing paths in court. I was confronting the monster who took my life from me for more than a year and almost killed my daughter. I prayed to God to give me the strength to do this for my son. I still had faith that people could change. After all, I had changed so very much that I didn't feel I had the right to pass judgment over past sins. I would give this a chance.

We went—me, Derrick and the boys. Horace greeted us warmly with hugs all around and acted like nothing had ever gone wrong. "This is all I want; I miss my family," he professed. "Do you think we can ever be together again?"

I may be forgiving, but I'm not crazy.

"That will never happen," I said firmly. "I'm here for the kids, so they can know their whole family." And that was a big part of my reason for going. The kids hadn't seen any of the relatives on their father's side for years. Horace's parents were there with Horace that day, as well as his extended family from New Orleans, making the visit a small family reunion. And I was happy the boys got to know their roots on that side and fill the void of their ancestry, since they could no longer remember New Orleans and their father. I had not kept anything from them and had told them in simple terms about what their father had done to them as babies, but that abuse was only an abstract concept to a ten- and eleven-year-old.

I didn't take Shaniqua that first time. Horace asked to see her. The last time he'd seen her, she'd been on life support in a hospital. That memory for me was still raw. I spent months agonizing after he asked me to see her. Eventually, I decided that if God had given me another chance with my kids, maybe He was giving that same chance to Horace. My parents were against it, but they respected my decision, and I let Horace meet his daughter. It was still a cautious meeting. I was there the whole time. Unlike with the boys, Shaniqua did not know what her biological father had done to her. She didn't know her condition was a result of his behavior, and to her, her daddy was Derrick.

Horace and his family embraced her when they saw her, now a nine-year-old. "She's so beautiful!" they said. And they were right. Her little body, all healed now, hinted at how gorgeous she'd be as an adult, which of course allowed everyone to ignore what had been done to her ability to use that body, and what had been done to the mind within it.

Horace embraced her tightly when he first saw her, and he cried. Shaniqua, for her part, didn't do anything. She had no idea who this man was or how he'd contributed to her life. Horace was a stranger to her. In her mind, the men who raised her—her grandfather, her uncle, and Derrick—were the ones that were important to her. She knew the word *father* and that she and her brothers shared the same one, but the word didn't have much meaning for her when it came to the man who shared her DNA.

Throughout my story, I haven't talked much about Shaniqua. Partly that's because of the painful nature of her story, and partly that's because she lived a lot of her childhood in other households. But one of the big lessons I learned from her was not to give up, and not to accept the narrative of others. After she'd healed from her injuries and the doctors determined her level of cerebral palsy— that she'd never be able to walk again, that she'd never communicate clearly—some might have accepted that fate as part of God's punishment. But I couldn't. My family and I couldn't. After we brought her home, we'd take her out of her tiny wheelchair built for a three-year-old and support her as we walked her about the room in her braces. It took years before she could get around on her own.

Kenneth never really warmed to Horace after that first reunion, but Junior still carried a torch for the relationship he wanted to have with his real dad. As I had done in my youth, Junior rebelled until he got his way. I allowed Junior to go live with Horace for a while, about three months after that first meeting.

It was one of the worst decisions I ever made.

Horace, tuning into Junior's difference, punished the boy for it, as I would later find out. "I didn't raise a sissy," he'd yell at Junior, and he'd try to beat it out of him. He wound up treating Junior so horribly during his stay there that he had a mental breakdown.

Horace put him in an in-patient mental health facility where they diagnosed him as bipolar and schizophrenic and treated him with psychiatric drugs. When I found out, I was livid. Junior had no such issues with me. He was still a child. But the authorities wouldn't allow me to see Junior because the court had mandated "treatment" for him. When I was finally able to get him out, he was a zombie, on a cocktail of medications. I didn't know who my son was anymore. And the court wouldn't let me bring him back to Dallas. All this within only months of finding Horace again.

All this so I could learn the hard lesson again: leopards can't change their spots, and some monsters are just monsters.

An Ending

In 2007, two years after I found Horace, while I was still working for Aetna, I got a call from Social Security. "Horace has listed these three children as his," the operator said, rattling off the kids' names. "Is that correct?"

"Yes," I replied, baffled, as up to this point I hadn't received a dime in child support.

"He's been approved for disability," the operator continued, "and because he must pay child support, here is your allotted monthly amount of that disability payment for your children."

I'd like to think, on his deathbed, Horace was trying to make something right by penning his kids' names on his disability application. I know sometimes a monster is just a monster, but I want to believe my young self saw something worth loving in him all those years ago.

Horace never took accountability specifically for his actions. He did, however, apologize as a whole, and said he'd never been the same after losing his first family. He'd moved on after the divorce and had another son named Dominique who looks just like his siblings. We found that brother through a cousin, and all the siblings were able to connect after Horace's funeral.

Six months after Social Security called me, I got another call. This one was from his mother. Horace wasn't doing too well. He'd ignored his diabetes, and parts of his body now had gangrene. I learned this from his mother because I'd stopped communicating with him after the trouble with Junior.

I told his mom we'd be praying, and I'd check with the kids to see if they wanted to see him, though I didn't think they would. I kept my word and offered the kids the chance to connect with him. They were good without him now, having experienced him up close. We were done. I was at peace with this. I'd done all I felt I had to. And at this point, Derrick was daddy.

Not long after that, Lorraine called again, crying this time. Horace was dead! She wanted me to send the boys down to Baton Rouge to help her process the death of her son.

"I'll let them know and see if they want to go," I hedged.

"No, you don't understand," she wailed. "I can't do anything. I can't pick out flowers. I can't pick the casket. I can't write the obituary. The boys are the only ones I have now!" Horace was her only child, and she desperately wanted to see a small piece of him again. Her mother's love melted me—no matter how bad the offspring, a mother's love is pure—and I told her I'd do what I could.

Derrick and I sat the kids down and told them their father had died. We asked if they wanted to go to the funeral. They said they did, so we found out the details of when and where and headed to Baton Rouge, Louisiana.

Lorraine hadn't been lying. No obituary had been done. No casket had been picked. No photos had been loaded for the funeral service. Everything was still up in the air. So Derrick and I spent the next forty-eight hours making the final decisions that would bury my first husband and pay tribute to his death. The irony of it all is not lost on me.

Before the funeral, Lorraine asked Derrick and me to sit in the back so that we didn't disrespect the family. "Absolutely," I replied. "Gladly. I don't do funerals anyway."

At their request, the kids rode in the limousine to the church with Horace's family, but all three refused to get out of the car without Derrick. "They're asking for their dad!" we were told by a frantic relative on my cell phone. We went to the limo to get the kids. I'm not sure what happened in there, but Junior was staring off into space, lost in his own thoughts. Shaniqua clung to Derrick like a lifeline. But Kenneth, once he saw us, was able to put on a brave face and get out of the car. We headed toward the back of the church, but the family now wanted us in the front seats with the kids. I let Kenneth sit next to his grandmother, him being the strongest at the moment. Junior was still in his own world next to me, and Shaniqua sat in Derrick's lap.

They asked the kids to say a few words. Kenneth, now twelve years old, who'd had his umbilical cord burnt off and feet scarred because the man lying in state thought he was illegitimate, was the only one who got up. He recited from Ecclesiastes 3:1-9 of the New Living Translation: "To everything there is a season, and a time to every purpose under heaven...a time to get, and a time to lose; a time to keep, and a time to cast away...a time to rend, and a time to sew; a time to keep silence, and a time to speak...all go unto one place; all are of the dust, and all turn to dust again." I was so proud of him. I'd read that passage to him numerous times, and now I knew he understood it. He understood that nobody was perfect.

When he was done, with the pride of a man radiating from his slim boy body, he turned to gaze on his deceased father and stated clearly, almost triumphantly, "In spite of what you did, I will still carry your last name."

So in the end, Kenneth was the one who spoke on behalf of his siblings for his father. I didn't know whether to smile or cry. I might have done a bit of both. Then they loaded Horace up to take him to the cemetery.

A

Homegoing Celebration

For

Brother Horace Yarbrough Kennedy, Sr.

Sunrise
September 26, 1970

23rd Psalm

Sunset
September 15, 2007

Saturday, September 22, 2007
12:00 Noon

"The Lord Is My Shepherd, I Shall Not Want"
Psalm 23:1

Gordon Feltus Lazard Cathedral
Church Of God In Christ
8930 Plank Road
Baton Rouge, LA. 70811

Bishop James Earl Gordon
Officiant

Because that particular gravesite sits on a swamp, we had to lay his body to rest in a unique way, but it was normal for Louisianna: they can't dig into the ground because the holes fill with water from the high water table. So they build tombs above ground to mark the dead. The tombs are big affairs compared with normal gravestones, and they cost a lot because of the sheer amount of stone that must be shaped, transported, and erected. It had been raining in Baton Rouge that day, so the ground at the graveyard was soggier than usual. Everyone had to track through mud, heat, bugs, and more mud in their shiny church shoes to get to Horace's final resting place. I said a quick prayer to keep whatever animals were out there off of me. The whole walk felt like a metaphor.

I didn't feel much when Horace's body was finally laid to rest. *Ashes to ashes, dust to dust. I forgive you,* I thought at the thing that was no longer my first husband, the man I'd loved and feared and who had altered my life forever. I put aside my pride and buried him with honor. I was now free of him...and not.

Though I may have buried his body and he could no longer hurt me and my family physically, the scars he left on my soul, I know now, will never completely go away. That kind of deep mental and emotional anguish sticks around long after any physical scars have faded, and you have to work at them, feel them, live with them hidden inside you for a long time before, one day, you take a look at your pain again and realize the hurt is now small enough that you can bring it out in the open for others to see it and know it without it looking so scary. At that moment, you can release it, like opening a fist and letting the dirty, crumpled feather you were holding drift away on the next breeze. That's when you finally feel like you've paid the last penny you owe to fate, and you are free.

It took more bumps along the road of life to process the feelings Horace's brief and chaotic reentry into our lives would bring up. And while that was happening, other hurdles came up to help me gain perspective. One of which nearly killed me.

Yet Another Chance

An occupational hazard of working as a physician liaison is that you're always too aware of how many people are sick, injured, or dying. In 2018 there seemed to be more than the normal number of people dying from brain aneurysms, or brain bleeds, in our area. Although I was aware of that, I didn't immediately think, *I have a brain bleed*, when I developed a horrible headache.

We'd just entered the church to attend the Woman Thou Art Loosed conference at the Potter's House. While going into the VIP area, my head started hurting like never before. A friend was getting ready to escort me into the sanctuary when it hit me. The headache pounded in my head so bad I asked them to grab me some medicine.

All I could do was pray. I asked God to please not let me be having an aneurysm.

I started feeling weak and nauseous. I headed to the restroom and immediately started vomiting. I called my husband. "Baby, something's not right. I don't feel good." Looking back, I realize that was an understatement.

He immediately left the BBQ shop and came to get me. Meanwhile, my friend found me in the restroom, and before I knew what was happening, an ambulance was there ready to take me to the emergency room because my blood pressure was through the roof.

But Derrick had arrived at the church too. He and Christy loaded me up in our truck. I passed out and lost consciousness in Christy's arms. All I can remember her saying is, "Jesus."

At Charlton Methodist Hospital, they took me to get a CT scan. I hadn't even made it back the to ER room they had for me when a doctor came my way. The look in his eyes immediately told me something was wrong. I asked him to go get my husband before revealing to me what they had seen in the scan. He did.

"This is not good," he said when Derrick was with me. "She has a brain bleed."

My husband called one of my good physician friends, and he ended up talking to the attending physician, which helped get us some kind of clarity. Almost immediately, I was transferred to another hospital and placed in the ICU. They did another CT scan.

This showed a hemorrhage. They were going to have to do surgery on my brain.

I knew what that meant: I might never be able to speak clearly again. I might need some form of physical therapy. I might die.

In fact, the odds were that I would die.

I prayed. Derrick prayed. My family and friends prayed. My children never left my side. The doctors wanted to do an angiogram, where they insert a tiny camera inside you to see what's going on, before going straight into brain surgery. When they went in, they noticed the bleeding had stopped.

And yes, I believe what happened next is proof that prayer works: not only did I survive, but I didn't need surgery. I stayed in the ICU for a little over a week. The doctors released me with trepidation, and I admit, I went home with some caution. I took a few weeks off from work to rest and completely recover, and unintentionally to open my eyes. I was amazed by the number of people who dropped off casseroles to my house, who came by to see if there was anything they could do to help my family, or who reached out to let us know they were there if we needed anything. I was equally amazed to notice who did none of those things.

I have many "friends" but far fewer friends. That was something I learned in the days following my brain bleed. All those "friends" I'd supported and cared for, who I would have done anything for, didn't even think about having my back during my time of need. Like the snakes back in prison. Only these people thought they were better than any inmate.

I didn't let it bother me too long. There was a more important lesson for me to learn from this experience. My brain had miraculously healed on its own. God wanted me to live. I knew that now. But why? What was I to do with my life that God felt was so important that I needed to survive the wilderness Horace had dragged me into and now this: something that was killing too many other young people?

I knew the answer would one day come. In the interim, I got busy being the best Katrina I could be. The best mom, the best wife, the best me in whatever activity I was in. And yes, I kind of forgot to find the answer to that question: why had God spared me?

Then Covid-19 hit, and I learned my answer. Every day going into the hospital where I worked, where death just seemed to be waiting for everybody, that question reared up once again, so loud I couldn't ignore it. *What good am I really doing?* That was when I sunk into a depression and started having nightmares, and Derrick forced me to take a break and clear my mind.

At my mother's house, while spending time in her grounding chair out in the yard, in the peace and quiet, I asked God for guidance.

God saves all of us for a reason. I felt God had saved me three times already—putting me in jail to escape Horace's violence, healing a brain bleed, and keeping me healthy despite being on the front line of medical workers during Covid.

I realized He didn't lead me through all those challenges to be silent about what I'd learned from them. Either I'd gone through everything to be silent, or I'd gone through everything to be a guiding light on the other side. Maybe, by sharing my story, I could provide hope, inspiration, and perseverance to someone else. To quote Miles Monroe again, "The graveyard is the richest place on Earth because it's filled with unfulfilled potential." I didn't want to take my secrets to the grave. I'd paid dearly for them, and if they could do good for someone else, let them have them. And since some expiration dates come much sooner than others, as the pandemic had taught me, why not share this knowledge now? Was I going to walk in my purpose or keep things to myself?

If just one person is inspired to keep going because of my story, then all that pain is worth it. I've done what I'm here to do.

My Season, My Purpose, My Story

God brings the seasons, but we determine how we live them. You might have highs and lows, as I have had, but you have to live in the season you're in—fully, unapologetically. Maybe this season you get to travel a lot. Maybe next season you won't. Maybe this season you strike it rich. Maybe the next you lose it all. Regardless of the season you're in, it's up to you to make the best of it. It's up to you to say that you're going to keep going when you don't feel like going or when you don't feel there's even a place to go to.

People say to me a lot now, "I wish I was like you. You have this perfect life." But they don't know the price I had to pay to get that life. The things I had to accept or forgive to keep living. Their adoration sits uncomfortably with me because if they knew my real story, I doubt they'd want to live it, not even for a nice house and a Range Rover.

I think this message is important: the price of a perfect-looking life is seldom seen. Real stories are not displayed on social media. We often only project what we want people to see, what we think they'll like. For any number of reasons, the real story of a life is often hidden.

But I've come to realize the journey, as well as the happy ending, is important for people to see.

It's important to see Cinderella in the ashes before she meets her fairy godmother.

It's important to see Snow White eat the poison apple before she gets kissed by her prince.

It's important to see Little Red Riding Hood get eaten by the wolf before she springs out of his cut-open belly to exclaim, "It was so dark in there!"

It's important because some of the people who see those stories are going through their own wilderness, and they want to know they can make it to the other side.

At the end of the day, I think everyone ends up in some sort of prison, whether those chains are mental or physical or spiritual.

We're all restrained by something, prevented from being our true selves. But we can't wait for a rescuer, a prince, or a divine hand to pluck us out of our darkness. We got into that wilderness somehow, and if we found a way in, we can find a way out again.

Freedom from my pain, to me, means being able to tell my story myself, without caring what other people will think or say about it. Freedom is being able to walk into what I am today. Freedom is being able to say to my doubters and detractors, "I survived."

That, to me, is being free.

Nobody's life is perfect, even when all signs finally point to the fantasy fulfilled. We all have to make peace with the hands we're dealt and love ourselves and our children for who we, and they, are. Even now, my life is not all perfect. There are still aspects of myself and my family I wrestle with behind the scenes. There are still new prices to be paid and struggles to get through.

The fight for freedom is never-ending.

It's up to us to control our own destinies. If others author our stories, what does that do to them? What's left out or misinterpreted? What boxes are checked, or not?

We are stories, not statistics. We must write our own narratives. We have the pen, the ink, and the paper. And so we write. Each chapter is different, and we get to write the moral at the end.

And something else: life stories don't stay the same. Each chapter is a chance for a new tale to be added to your book. We don't have to get stuck in our old stories, no matter how many sad ones we write.

I know where I came from. I know what I did, and what I did not do, in my life. I fully embrace those parts of me, those stories, because they brought me to this page, this season, this purpose.

I also know I'm still writing my story. I now run a BBQ restaurant with Derrick, and I'm still working in the medical field to support him as he fulfills one of his dreams. I'm now developing a curriculum for inmates who are behind bars, supporting other women who are living similar stories to mine, to help them turn the page. I still make trips back to Mexico to see my mother's family, so I don't forget where I came from and how far I've traveled. I don't want to forget, in my current comfortable season, how everything can be taken from you. And that, even in those moments, you keep writing because unlike a fairy tale, in real life there's always a next chapter.

That's the beauty of writing your own story. Every turn of the page reveals a new leaf of paper that is clean and bright and mercifully blank. Only when you touch that pen down do you leave a mark, and as long as you hold tight to that pen, you can shape that mark any way you like.

Acknowledgments

If I can be real, this book was very difficult to write. The trauma that arose trying to write something that I was determined to bury for twenty-eight years was extremely difficult. I've had so many triggers that arose by reliving my past, BUT GOD. Without Him and the people He placed in my life, this book would not have been possible.

To Derrick, my husband, my ride or die, my everything, thank you for loving me the way you do. Thank you for supporting me. Thank you for believing in me. Thank you for covering me, and most of all, thank you for being a daddy to my heartbeats. I'm better because of you, and I absolutely love doing this thing called life with you. Thank you for being my answered prayer.

In memory of my dad, Louis C. Rogers. I get it now. I understand why you had to leave. I just hate that you are not here. I pray that I have made you proud. Please continue to watch over me, my auntie, and my brothers.

To my parents, Stanley and Maria Mack, thank you for literally sacrificing your lives for me and my children. You both have been with me through every valley and through every mountaintop experience. Words cannot express how thankful and grateful I am for your endless love.

Tony, I can never repay you for all that you have done for me. Not only have you shared my journey with me, but you have always been my rock. Thank you for never leaving my side, for always being there, and last but not least, thank you for being my keeper. We made it, big brother! We made it!

LC, thank you, little brother, for giving me your blessings. I love you and appreciate you. We are all proud of you and are so thankful that you're in our lives. Let's continue to make Dad proud.

Jr, Kenneth, Shaniqua, and Janae, you four are my heroes. You are the true definition of what resilience looks like. Thank you for still loving me through my darkest moments and never giving up on me. I am because of y'all. Thank you for letting me know that you will win if you don't quit! I'm so blessed that God allowed me to be your mother. We made it!!!

To my daughters, Dekyra and De'nia, thank you for doing this thing called life with me. Never forget who you are and whose you are. Always remember that the sky is the limit. I love y'all.

To my Little Heart Beats (my g-babies), thank you for bringing so much joy into my life.

Masa, we had countless hours together of dreaming, dancing, crying, and laughing only to make our dreams become a reality twenty-five years later. Man...I still can't believe it! Thank you for being that true ride or die.

Christy, thank you for seeing something in me that I didn't see in myself. I will forever be grateful to you. I love you.

Evangelist Andria, my spiritual mentor and sister for over twenty years, I appreciate you more than you know. Thank you for being my spiritual covering. I'm so grateful to God for you!

To *mi familia*: Connie, Tia, Liz, Alexa, Peyton, Nathaniel, Louie, Cecilia, my *tías* and *tíos*, JC, Lisa, Katrina, Chocka, and Julie, thanks for being an inspiration in my life and pushing me to be better.

And finally, to my God-sent team:

Lisa Shiroff founder of Tasfil Concierge Publishing. You were such a joy to work with. Thank you for pushing me to go into deeper depths and challenging me throughout the manuscript. You brought out a story that has been buried for the last twenty-eight years. I couldn't have done this without you. You are who made this book possible.

Neshe Conley of NC Public Relations. I'm so happy I said yes to the meeting! I'm so blessed to have the best SM manager. You have been so instrumental in every aspect of Lady K. Thank you for believing in the vision and laying a foundation.

Ron Sanders of Ron K. Sanders Photography. Not only are you an amazing photographer, but you are also my brother from another mother. Thank you for always being there, for believing in my vision, and for pushing me for greater.

VV, thank you for keeping me on my p's and q's as only you can do! Thank you for making sure there were no edits, being my right and left brain, while keeping my joy instilled in Jesus throughout this process. I'm so grateful that God allowed our paths to cross.

Ron Flanagan, a.k.a. Ron the VP, thank you for taking the vision and bringing it to life with your skill and talent.

Reyna Joye Banks, CEO and Founder of FHG Entertainment LLC, Thank you for your yes! I can't thank you enough for taking my dream and running with it. You saw it; you believed in it, and the rest is history! Thank you for being my midwife in the birthing room.

And thank you to the beta readers! Your input is much appreciated!

About the Author

Author, coach, mom, wife, motivational speaker, and prison reform advocate Katrina Harris is on a mission to help women tap into their potential, overcome adversity, and step into their power so that they can become the people they were destined to be. She believes every individual has the power to shape their own narrative and rise above their circumstances. Through her podcasts, prison outreach initiatives, and coaching, she inspires, educates, and motivates single moms, domestic abuse survivors, and women and men with rough upbringings to reclaim their power and create a life they love.

You can learn more about Katrina at https://www.ladykharris.com/

Made in the USA
Middletown, DE
07 September 2024

60528414R00120